Middle Ground Prepping
A Sensible Approach

by

Jim Serre

Edited by: Janet L. Gill
                Carol A. Serre

Cover Design: Argus Design Group

Table of Contents

Introduction

On October 17, 1989 at 5:04 PM PST, during game three of the World Series between the San Francisco Giants and Oakland Athletics, the Loma Prieta earthquake hit the San Francisco bay area with a magnitude of 6.9. The quake was responsible for 63 deaths and 3,757 injuries in the affected areas. Due to the sports coverage of the 1989 World Series, it became the first major earthquake in the United States that was broadcast live on national television.

The bombing of the Alfred P. Murrah Federal Building in downtown Oklahoma City on April 19, 1995 killed 168 people and injured more than 680. In 2001, the United States was attacked by four separate suicide bombers in commercial aircraft as we watched one of the planes hit the World Trade Center on live television. 2,977 victims died as a result of this single day attack on U.S. soil. 2005 brought unimaginable suffering to thousands of gulf coast residents as a result of Hurricane Katrina and 1,836 perished. And Americans still did not fully understand the need to *prepare for the unexpected*®.

It was not until June 27, 2011 that the concept of "prepping" went main stream with the launch of the TV series "Doomsday Preppers." It started out simple enough trying to show how some folks were preparing for future disasters. However, like most "reality" TV shows, in order to keep it interesting, the producers had to find more and more fanatical and "colorful" characters to showcase in each episode.

As the show progressed, and in the follow up series "Doomsday Preppers, Bugged Out" there was a definite focus on extreme preparedness efforts. While the motivations and preparations of the preppers shown were interesting and educational, their situations were not relatable to millions of Americans. How many of us live on 20 acres, have hundreds of thousands of dollars to spend on prepping structures and supplies, and have a bug-out cabin in the woods?

On the other end of the prepping spectrum are the millions of Americans who have done nothing to assemble emergency supplies to support themselves in case of local civil unrest, economic collapse or regional weather disasters. As evidenced by several surveys since Hurricane Katrina, only around 30% of Americans say their disaster preparedness is adequate. Their plan must be to depend on the generosity of the rest of us to support the Red Cross (with cash donations) and FEMA (with our tax donations).

Somewhere in between fanatical doomsday prepping and those with nothing lies "middle ground prepping." Middle ground prepping is a concept that provides a measured and reasonable response to preparing for impending emergencies or disasters in order to protect yourself and your family. While survivalists require top of the line survival gear, middle ground prepping depends on gear and supplies that are of reasonable quality and will function properly during what we hope is a once in a lifetime emergency.

This book will delve into the history of prepping in the United States to understand why we prep and how we prep. The modern psychology of prepping, and how to prepare for future disasters using the more reasonable concept of middle ground prepping available to all citizens will be examined.

Chapter 1 – Why We Prepare

In 1803, responses to disasters in America took a significant turn, starting the pattern of federal involvement that continues today. After the first of three great fires to sweep through Portsmouth, New Hampshire, recovery efforts severely taxed community and state resources. An appeal to Congress brought the first piece of national disaster legislation, The Congressional Act of 1803. This allowed the federal government to provide disaster funds to the City of Portsmouth.

On September 8, 1900 a Category 4 hurricane hit Galveston, TX and completely submerged Galveston Island. Including hurricane Katrina, it was the deadliest and second costliest hurricane in U.S. history. The hurricane caused great loss of life with the estimated death toll between 6,000 and 12,000 individuals. [1] Nearly half the homes were swept out of existence, and not a single building went undamaged. The Galveston hurricane was a far greater disaster than better-known events such as the Chicago fire of 1871, which killed 250 people, the 1906 San Francisco earthquake, which killed 480, or the Johnstown (PA) flood in 1889, which claimed over 2,200 lives. Over the next century ad hoc legislation would be passed more than 100 times in response to hurricanes, earthquakes, floods and other natural disasters.

The concept of our modern government trying to help the populous prepare for the worst continued with national civil defense initiatives. Civil Defense truly began to come of age, both worldwide and in the United States, during World War I — although it was usually referred to as civilian defense. This was formalized with the creation of the Council of National Defense on August 29, 1916. Civil defense responsibilities at the federal level were vested in this council, with subsidiary councils at the state and local levels providing additional support. As the United States had little threat of a direct attack on its shores, the organization instead "maintained anti-saboteur vigilance, encouraged men to join the armed forces, facilitated the implementation of the draft, participated in Liberty Bond drives, and helped to maintain the morale of the soldiers." [2] This freedom to focus beyond air raid attacks gave United States civil defense a much broader scope than elsewhere. However, with the end of military conflict, the activities of the Council of National Defense were suspended. [3]

Then came the Great Depression (1929-39) which was the deepest and longest-lasting economic downturn in the history of the Western industrialized world. In the United States, the Great Depression began soon after the stock market crash of October 1929. Over the next several years, consumer spending and investment dropped, causing steep declines in industrial output and rising levels of unemployment as failing companies laid off workers. By 1933, some 13 to 15 million Americans were unemployed and nearly half of the country's banks had failed. Though the relief and reform measures put into place by President Franklin D. Roosevelt helped lessen the worst effects of the Great Depression in the 1930s, the economy would not fully turn around until after 1939, when World War II kicked American industry into high gear. During this decade, times were tough, and most people learned how to make do with what they had. For 76 million Baby Boomers, those people were our grandparents and parents!

Those born between 1928 and 1945 were part of what was called the "Silent Generation. The term Silent Generation was coined by Time magazine in a November 1951 article as the group was coming of age. The article described them as "working fairly hard and saying almost nothing," one that "does not issue manifestos, make speeches or carry posters." The Great Depression had significant influence on this group as they generally worked hard, rarely wasted food, and learned to take care of themselves.[4]

The Great Depression was also a time for learning new self-serving skills like sewing, barbering, carpentry, plumbing, auto maintenance and welding, gardening and canning, and recycling. Why? Because folks couldn't afford to buy a new shirt when it was torn or a button fell off. They had to keep that shirt and fix it somehow. They learned to cut hair for the entire family. They fixed leaky roofs, broken water pumps, and cars that wouldn't start with parts they could make or repair. But gardening was perhaps the most valuable skill of all. By starting a garden, in what little space they could find, they produced food they could eat and they only needed the seeds! Everyone had a garden and maybe a couple trees to provide much needed fruit, nuts, vegetables, and legumes. With all the economic turmoil in the country people started saving items like scrap metal instead of throwing it out in case it could be of use someday (the beginning of recycling).

Another way these depression families made due was the use of lower quality foods. Soups, stews, and casseroles became popular household meals that stretched the family food budget. Folks learned how to do without and adapted many of their food ingredients when cooking. For example

- Crisco was less expensive than butter.
- Oscar Meyer Wieners replaced more costly sausages.
- Maxwell House Sanka coffee was an option to whole bean coffees.
- Heinz Ketchup was used to make a simple tomato soup.
- Underwood Deviled Ham was a substitute for fresh lunch meat.
- Carnation evaporated milk replaced fresh milk.
- Honey, molasses and corn sweeteners replaced sugar which came at a premium.

So as a result of the Great Depression, and to simply survive, people began to put in a coffee can what little money they could save to be used for a rainy day. They threw out very little and used what little garbage they had to create compost for their gardens. They stockpiled foods that they grew by canning, used stored rainwater to water gardens all summer long, and generally took care of themselves. Often times, neighbors could barter their skills to help one another out. One might fix the wiring in a neighbor's lamp in return for three potatoes. Neighbors would help neighbors and folks knew who had certain skills that could be useful to them.

In broad terms, "prepping" means planning for self-sufficiency and security in case a severe disaster, martial law, or war was to occur on home soil. People were already prepping — but they didn't call it that yet. For now, most preps were focused on protecting their family from a continued, or another, financial meltdown.

More government support

Being in a state of readiness can also be traced back to Great Britain during the 'blitz'. Between September 7, 1940 and May 21, 1941, the German 'Blitzkrieg' ("lightning war") conducted regular and major aerial bombing raids on British cities during the Second World War. Starting on September 7, 1940, London alone was bombed by the Luftwaffe for 57 consecutive nights. [5]

The British learned quickly that they needed to prepare every day for the nightly raids to ensure their survival. Everyone had to be prepared to shelter, to wear a gas mask, to make their home as safe as possible, and to be fully prepared for the worse scenarios that could happen to them. This lesson would soon be brought to the U.S.

As World War II began, most folks in America didn't really trust banks and certainly not the stock market!

Most were used to austerity and had no problem sacrificing a little for the war effort. As the war began President Roosevelt reactivated the Council of National Defense (CND). However, the idea of local and state councils bearing a significant burden became viewed as untenable and more responsibility was vested at the federal level with the creation of the Office of Civilian Defense (OCD) within the Office of Emergency Planning (OEP) [6].

These organizations and others worked together to mobilize the civilian population in response to the threat of attack in the United States. The Civil Air Patrol (CAP) was created just days before the attack on Pearl Harbor. The patrol used commissioned civilian pilots to patrol the U.S. coastline and borders and engage in search and rescue missions. Thousands of volunteer members answered America's call to national service and sacrifice by accepting and performing critical wartime missions. Assigned to the War Department under the jurisdiction of the Army Air Corps, the contributions of Civil Air Patrol, including logging more than 500,000 flying hours, sinking two enemy submarines, and saving hundreds of crash victims during World War II, are well documented. After the war, a thankful nation understood that the Civil Air Patrol could continue providing valuable services to both local and national agencies. On July 1, 1946, President Harry Truman signed Public Law 476 incorporating Civil Air Patrol as a benevolent, nonprofit organization. On May 26, 1948, Congress passed Public Law 557 permanently establishing Civil Air Patrol as the auxiliary of the new U.S. Air Force. Three primary mission areas were set forth at that time: aerospace education, cadet programs, and emergency services. The patrol is still in existence today and most well known for their search and rescue operations locating missing aircraft and persons.

The Civil Defense Corps, run by the OCD, organized approximately 10 million volunteers who trained to fight fires, decontaminate after chemical weapon attacks, provide first aid, and other duties. [6] The Corps was not unlike the modern day Community Emergency Response Team (CERT) program which will be discussed later. During World War II, the nation's civil defense activities expanded but still included those initiated during WW I. During the Second World War, civil defense in the U.S saw an even greater use of rationing, recycling, and anti-saboteur vigilance than was seen in WW I. As the threat of air raids or invasions in the United States seemed less likely during the war, the focus of the Civil Defense Corps on air raid drills and patrols of the border declined, but the other efforts continued. While civil defense efforts lost their luster in late 1945 as the war ended, the U.S. did not completely dismiss them as they had after World War I.

Then in 1949, the old Soviet Union successfully tested an atomic bomb, and the U.S. domination in nuclear weaponry was in doubt. Not only did this event alter foreign policy but it also gave Americans a true sense of vulnerability. The country began to fear that they could be attacked by the very weapon they created several years earlier. Bowing to social and political pressure, President Truman started to postulate how a civil defense program could be structured for an atomic attack. Key lessons from the German Blitzkrieg in Great Britain, taught the U.S. that they too must prepare citizens.

On September 30, 1950 Congress passed the Federal Disaster Relief Act, which was designed primarily to allow the federal government to provide some limited assistance to the states during times of disaster.

In December 1950, Truman created the Federal Civil Defense Administration (FCDA), the Homeland Security Department of its day, which became an official government agency in January 1951 within what was called the Office of Emergency Management (OEM). The role of the FCDA was to educate and reassure the country that there were ways to survive an atomic attack from the Soviet Union. They had the authority for planning, sheltering, and evacuation and support to states and localities with planning, technical guidance and assistance, training, and fifty-fifty matching grants for equipment.[7] In its early years, the agency attempted to put forward a comprehensive nationwide plan for fallout shelters, but confusion over goals led to insufficient budgets passing Congress, and in later years, the agency focused on evacuation as a strategy.[2] Therefore, the FCDA was involved in only limited construction of fallout shelters and the publishing of publicity materials.

The FCDA commissioned a university study on how to achieve "emotion management" during the early days of the Cold War. One of their approaches was to involve schools. Teachers in selected cities were encouraged to conduct air raid drills where they would suddenly yell, "Drop!" and students were expected to kneel down under their desks with their fingers interlocked to cover their heads. New York City spent $159,000 on 2.5 million identification bracelets, or dog tags, for students to wear at all times—with the unspoken purpose being that they would help distinguish children who were lost or killed in a nuclear explosion. [8] The next step was to promote these "preparedness" measures around the country, and the FCDA decided the best way to do that was to commission an educational film that would appeal to children.

In 1951, the agency awarded a contract for the production to a New York firm known as Archer Films. The producers went to work on a script that would combine live actors and an animated turtle to encourage kids to duck down to the ground and get under some form of cover – a desk, a table or next to a wall – if they ever saw a bright flash of light. The flash would presumably be produced by an atomic blast. The hero of the film was the animated Turtle named Bert who wore a pith helmet and quickly ducked his head into his shell when a monkey in a tree set off a firecracker nearby. [9] The original nine minute black and white "Duck and Cover" video can be viewed here.

Original "Duck and Cover" poster

The movie *"Duck and Cover"* was completed in January 1952 and included the film in the "Alert America Convoy." This was a convoy of 10 trucks and trailers that toured the country for nine months in 1952. Each vehicle contained civil defense dioramas, posters, 3-D models, and a film theatre showing the movie and other educational movies. According to the FCDA, 1.1 million people eventually saw the convoy exhibits. At the same time, the movie was distributed to schools around the country. It was shown on television stations around the country and some educated guesses put the TV audience in the tens of millions. [9]

Between 1953 and 1958, there continued to be arguments over whether evacuation or sheltering would be the nation's policy regarding response to a nuclear attack. There was vigorous debate in Congress, in the Executive Branch, and even among individuals charged with the responsibility of managing civil defense programs. The general public had largely grown tired of civil defense due to the political face put on by the Eisenhower Administration about maintaining a peaceful co-existence with the Russians. However, the development of intercontinental ballistic missile capability and the subsequent launch of the Sputnik satellite (October 4, 1957), along with the Soviet Union's explosion of a hydrogen bomb (August 12, 1953) once again fueled fears of the potential for a Russian attack on the United States. This time, however, the evacuation planners had to confront the fact that a Soviet missile could reach the U. S. in a few minutes, and that we may not have "several hours" to carry out an evacuation. [10]

The mushroom cloud from the Soviet's first hydrogen bomb test

Then in 1958 the FCDA was merged into the Office of Defense Mobilization (ODM). The ODM's function was to plan, coordinate, direct, and control all wartime mobilization activities of the federal government, including manpower, economic stabilization, and transport operations. The new entity became known as the Office of Civil and Defense Mobilization and functioned until 1961 when the office was re-designated as the Office of Emergency Planning.

If you are a little confused right now between all the various councils, departments, offices and corps, you are not alone. The entire country, including the government, was not sure which entity did what. Between the CND, OCD, OEP, CAP, CDC, FCDA, OEM, ODM, and OCDM; it was difficult to determine the exact purview of each government preparedness organization.

During this "Cold War" era, all of the media and government attention was focused on preparing for a nuclear attack. The mid 50's to the early 60's saw Americans building underground bunkers that promised to protect them from such an attack from Soviet bombers. Playing on the traditional imagery of women as domestic caretakers, the FCDA pitched advertisements for "Grandma's Pantry," a home shelter that women should stock with canned goods, first-aid kits, and flashlights. Commercial firms marketed a range of safe houses that ranged from a "$13.50 foxhole shelter" to a $5,000 "deluxe" model that included a phone, beds, toilets, and even a Geiger counter. [8] Canning foods and storing supplies were engrained in the minds of Depression children, so it all made sense to the Silent Generation.

In the early 1960's, The American Civil Defense Association (TACDA) was formed in response to our nations reliance on atomic weaponry as a centerpiece of foreign policy following World War II. But this was not a government agency, TACDA was a non-profit, non-political organization supported primarily by the American public. It still exists today to promote education, products, and resources that empower American citizens. TACDA provides a comprehensive understanding of reasonable preparedness strategies and techniques; promoting a self-reliant, pro-active approach to protecting individuals, families and communities in the event of nuclear, biological, chemical, or other man-made and natural disasters.

To this end, the association offers TACDA Academy which is an online collection of 17 different Civil Defense Basics including

- All Hazard Sheltering,
- Sanitation,
- Alternative Energy & Fuel,
- Medical Preparedness, and
- Post Event Survival.

After the Cuban Missile Crisis in October 1962, and the 1963 nuclear test-ban treaty between the U.S. and Russia, the "Cold War" and associated nuclear threat began to fade away from public concern. The prevailing sentiment was why did all those folks waste money to build a bomb shelter in their backyard? From this time on, the government mainly focused on helping citizens prepare for weather related disasters.

On April 1, 1979, President Jimmy Carter signed the executive order that created the modern Federal Emergency Management Agency (FEMA). FEMA's mission was to support citizens and first responders to ensure that as a nation we work together to build, sustain, and improve our capability to prepare for, protect against, respond to, recover from, and mitigate domestic disasters; whether natural or man-made, including acts of terror.

Then in 1985 the concept of widespread local volunteer emergency responders was implemented and developed by the Los Angeles Fire Department. The Whittier Narrows earthquake in 1987 underscored the area-wide threat of a major disaster in southern California. Further, it confirmed the need for training civilians to meet their own immediate needs. As a result, the LAFD created the Disaster Preparedness Division with the purpose of training citizens and private and government employees. By 1993, the Federal Emergency Management Agency had made the Community Emergency Response Team (CERT) program available nationwide. CERT is one of five federal programs promoted under the umbrella organization Citizen Corps. The Citizen Corps is a program under the Department of Homeland Security designed to provide training for the population of the United States to assist in the recovery after a disaster or terrorist attack. CERT and the Citizen Corps were transferred to the Office of Domestic Preparedness in August 2004. Currently, the Citizen Corps program is under the Department of Homeland Security.

While most communities use the CERT acronym, some may refer to their units as Neighborhood Emergency Response Teams (NERT), or Neighborhood Emergency Teams (NET). However, the CERT core curriculum for the basic course is composed of the following nine units usually consisting of 24 hours of lecture and practical exercises.

- **Unit 1**: Disaster Preparedness - Topics include identifying local disaster threats, disaster impact, mitigation, and preparedness concepts.
- **Unit 2**: Fire Safety - Students learn about fire chemistry, mitigation practices, hazardous materials identification, suppression options, and are introduced to the concept of size-up. Hands-on skills include using a fire extinguisher to suppress a live fire, and wearing basic protective gear.
- **Unit 3**: Disaster Medical Operations part 1 - Students learn to identify and treat certain life-threatening conditions in a disaster setting, as well as START (Simple Triage And Rapid Treatment) triage. Hands-on skills include performing head-tilt/chin-lift, practicing bleeding control techniques, and performing triage as an exercise.

- **Unit 4**: Disaster Medical Operations part 2 - Topics cover mass casualty operations, public health, assessing patients, and treating injuries. Students practice patient assessment, and various treatment techniques.
- **Unit 5**: Light Search and Rescue Operations - Size-up is expanded as students learn about assessing structural damage, marking structures that have been searched, search techniques, as well as rescue techniques and cribbing. Cribbing is the use of heavy timbers laid in layers at right angles to one another (cribs) to support heavy loads when extricating trapped victims. Hands-on activities include lifting and cribbing an object, and practicing rescue carries.
- **Unit 6**: CERT Organization - Students are introduced to several concepts from the Incident Command System and local team organization and communication is explained. Hands-on skills include a table-top exercise focusing on incident command and control.
- **Unit 7**: Disaster Psychology – Topics include responder well-being and dealing with victim trauma.
- **Unit 8**: Terrorism and CERT - Students learn how terrorists may choose targets, what weapons they may use, and identifying when weapons such as chemical, biological, radiological, nuclear, or explosive may have been deployed. Students learn about CERT roles in preparing for and responding to terrorist attacks.

- **Unit 9**: Course Review and Disaster Simulation - Students participate in a real-time practical disaster simulation where all the different skills taught are put to the test.

CERT command center and equipment staging

Some CERT units provide continuing and expanded training for their members that are pertinent to their local environment. For example, many units provide missing person search and rescue operations for local police and fire departments. Others in areas that are prone to flooding learn how to fill and stack sandbags. More advanced training in traffic control, crowd management, communications, the National Incident Management System (NIMS), water rescue, crime scene preservation, and medical operations is also available in many units. Most units train their medical members to be certified as Emergency

Medical Responders with basic life support skills and CPR. All CERT members are volunteers interested in learning to help themselves, their family, neighbors, communities and their state during a disaster. CERT units are generally associated with local fire or police departments and serve under their direction.

Terror comes to America

The United States had never been attacked and was never bombed as many thought we could have been during the Cold War. But religious fanatics and terrorists brought the fight to U.S. soil.

In mid-1981, Bhagwan Shree Rajneesh, an Indian mystic, guru and spiritual teacher relocated to the United States, where his followers established an intentional community (later known as Rajneeshpuram) near Antelope, Oregon south of The Dalles, Oregon. Almost immediately, the commune's leadership became embroiled in conflicts with local residents (primarily over land use), which were marked by hostility on both sides. [11] In 1984 Rajneesh followers conducted a bio-terror attack where 751 individuals in The Dalles, Oregon, United States, were given food poisoning through the deliberate contamination of salad bars at ten local restaurants with salmonella. The group had hoped to incapacitate the voting population of the city so that their own candidates would win the 1984 Wasco County elections. [12] The salmonella attack was the first confirmed instance of chemical (or biological) terrorism in the United States. [13]

On February 26, 1993, at 12:18 p.m., a Ryder rental truck with a terrorist bomb exploded in a parking garage of the World Trade Center in New York City, leaving a crater 60 feet wide and causing the collapse of several steel-reinforced concrete floors. Although the bomb failed to damage the main structure of the skyscrapers, six people were killed and more than 1,000 were injured. After the attack, authorities evacuated 50,000 people from the buildings, hundreds of whom were suffering from smoke inhalation. City authorities and the Federal Bureau of Investigation (FBI) undertook a massive manhunt for suspects, and within days several radical Islamic fundamentalists were arrested. In March 1994, Mohammed Salameh, Ahmad Ajaj, Nidal Ayyad, and Mahmoud Abouhalima were convicted by a federal jury for their role in the terrorist bombing.

Then, on April 19, 1995, the Alfred P. Murrah Federal Building in downtown Oklahoma City became the first domestic terrorist bomb attack in the U.S. The attack was carried out by Timothy McVeigh and Terry Nichols and the bombing killed 168 people [14] and injured more than 680 others. [15] Coincidentally, McVeigh drove the bomb in a van also rented from Ryder.

As a veteran and the result of the Cold War's end, McVeigh shifted his ideology from a hatred of foreign communist governments to a suspicion of the U.S. federal government. He especially hated President Bill Clinton who had successfully campaigned for the presidency on a platform of gun control. McVeigh, Nichols and their associates were deeply radicalized by such events as the August 1992 shoot-out between federal agents and survivalist Randy Weaver at his Idaho cabin, in which Weaver's wife and son were killed, and the April 19, 1993, inferno near Waco, Texas, in which 75 members of a Branch Davidian religious sect died. McVeigh planned an attack on the Murrah Building, because it housed regional offices of such federal agencies as the Drug Enforcement Agency, the Secret Service and the Bureau of Alcohol, Tobacco and Firearms and Explosives, the agency that had launched the initial raid on the Branch Davidian compound.[16] Domestic terrorism was now part of America's vernacular. However, the psyche of American Preppers was about to be changed forever.

Before 9/11 came 10/12. In the port of Aden, Yemen, on October 12, 2000, a small boat laden with 400-700 pounds of explosives was detonated next to the hull of the USS Cole while it was refueling. [17] The explosion created a 40-by-60-foot gash in the ship's port side. Seventeen sailors were killed and 39 were injured in the blast. It was subsequently learned that the attack was organized and directed by a terrorist organization known as al-Qaeda.

On September 11, 2001, 19 militants associated with the Islamic extremist group known as al-Qaeda, hijacked four airliners and carried out suicide attacks against targets in the United States. Two of the planes were flown into the towers of the World Trade Center in New York City, a third plane hit the Pentagon just outside Washington, D.C., and the fourth plane crashed in a field in Pennsylvania. Often referred to as "9/11", the attacks resulted in the death of 2,977 victims (not including terrorists), triggering major U.S. initiatives to combat terrorism. [18]

And most recently, on April 15, 2013, two home-made pressure cooker bombs were placed in backpacks and left on a crowded Boylston Street to explode during the finish of the Boston Marathon. At 2:49:43 pm EDT, the first bomb exploded and 13 seconds later a second bomb exploded about 630 feet away. The bombs killed three people and injured an estimated 264 others. [19] Dzhokhar Tsarnaev and his brother Tamerlan were motivated by extremist Islamic beliefs, and "were not connected to any known terrorist groups"; instead learning to build explosive weapons from an online magazine published by al-Qaeda affiliates in Yemen. [20]

In the past decade, there have also now been dozens of predatory "lone wolf" domestic terrorist attacks using mainly guns and knives in the U.S. Terrorism is no longer a concept to study, it is firmly entrenched in the minds and lexicon of Americans. Terrorist attacks could easily happen in our backyards with the proliferation of Islamic extremist sects in the Middle East.

What sayeth the Lord

It is ironic that a good deal of the history of prepping is also rooted in people's religious beliefs and their interpretation of some very old and thick religious books. Since the beginning of time, religion has been a big influence in people's need to *prepare for the unexpected*®. Biblical references include

- Galatians 6:5: "For each will have to bear his own load."
- Proverbs 6:6-11: "Go to the ant, O sluggard; consider her ways, and be wise. Without having any chief, officer, or ruler, she prepares her bread in summer and gathers her food in harvest. How long will you lie there, O sluggard? When will you arise from your sleep? A little sleep, a little slumber, a little folding of the hands to rest, and poverty will come upon you like a robber, and want like an armed man." This tells us to watch the ants (that do nothing but prepare for the future) and learn from their ways and become wise; that we should prepare like the ants do, without being told, because it is in our best interest.
- Proverbs 21:5: "The plans of the diligent lead surely to abundance, but everyone who is hasty comes only to poverty."
- Proverbs 21:20: "The wise store up choice food and olive oil, but fools gulp theirs down."
- Proverbs 22:3: "The prudent sees danger and hides himself, but the simple go on and suffer for it."
- Proverbs 27:12: "A prudent person foresees the danger ahead and takes precautions. The simpleton goes blindly on and suffers the consequences."

- Timothy 5:8: If anyone does not provide for his relatives, and especially for his immediate family, he has denied the faith and is worse than an unbeliever."

But it is probably The Church of Jesus Christ of Latter-day Saints that is the staunchest proponent of preparing for emergencies. Also known as the LDS Church and Mormons, they store food so that they can be prepared to care for themselves, their families, and their neighbors in case of an emergency. They further understand that basic human needs must be met before we can think about spiritual matters. Food storage ensures that those needs will be met. The "year's supply" of food that the Mormon Church is famous for is a counsel that is given to all members of the Mormon faith. There isn't a person out there that would not benefit from having such a backup supply on-hand. "Many more people could ride out the storm-tossed waves in their economic lives if they had their . . . supply of food . . . and were debt-free. Today we find that many have followed this counsel in reverse: they have at least a year's supply of debt and are food-free." [21]

Church World Service is an agency created in 1946, in the aftermath of World War II. Seventeen denominations came together "to do in partnership what none of us could hope to do as well alone." Their mission is to feed the hungry, clothe the naked, heal the sick, comfort the aged, and shelter the homeless before and after disasters. Today, the agency boasts 37 international member churches and actively promotes family and congregation preparedness through these churches. They do this with a resource document entitled, "Prepare to Care: Guide to Disaster Ministry In Your Congregation." The document discusses the need to conduct a local hazard assessment, create an emergency plan, stock supplies and training. [22]

Doomsday

Given the religious bent toward prepping and all the global concern over terrorism, economic collapse, and climate change; prepping was about to go mainstream. On June 27, 2011 a pilot TV program called "Doomsday Preppers" debuted on the National Geographic Channel. The program profiled various survivalists, or "Preppers", who were preparing to survive the various circumstances that may cause the end of civilization, including economic collapse, societal collapse, and electromagnetic pulses. The quality of their preparation was graded by a consulting company called Practical Preppers, who provide analysis and recommendations for improvements in their prepping efforts.

After watching the first episode, people were yelling "You're crazy! That will never happen!" and "You're preparing for your preposterous doomsday scenario all wrong!" This dichotomy intensified even more when a Southern man's pastor prayed over his food storage supplies and extensive arsenal. He was preparing for civil unrest caused by hyper-inflation. While praying over food supplies is normal, when a pastor started blessing the participant's arsenal including Molotov cocktails, it was a bit much!

The religious beliefs of those highlighted on the show were not apparent, and some appeared to have no religious connections at all. What was most troubling about many of the people featured on this show was their lack of generosity toward others. To the show's credit, it has featured exceptions to this selfish mentality. One woman preparing for a pandemic flu assembled hundreds of pandemic safety kits and distributed them to her neighbors. This approach was in part self-interested, but also included the knowledge that communities matter and other people matter. The show's "experts" frequently suggest that Preppers get their neighbors involved so they would not have to work alone during a disaster scenario (which varies, but includes both natural and social disasters).

Doomsday Preppers has received varied reviews. Neil Genzlinger in The New York Times condemned it as an "absurd excess on display and what an easy target the Prepper worldview is for ridicule," noting, "how offensively anti-life these shows are, full of contempt for humankind." [23] Genzlinger also believed that what these people really wanted is "a license to open fire." Nevertheless, "The program has been a ratings bonanza, with a 60-percent male audience, with an average age of 44." [24] Doomsday Preppers is the network's most-watched series and the highest-rated show in the history of the National Geographic Channel. [25]

The idea started out simple enough with common people trying to prepare for something bad that could happen. As the show progressed over several seasons, the focus shifted to Preppers with bigger and better preps. For example in Season 3, "Take Our Country Back," one individual built a fortress on his 80-acre estate in the high desert of Oregon. The property has, among other things, a 3,000-square-foot greenhouse, an artificial lake, infrared cameras and a high-tech software system, and 30 bugout vehicles (for use when they need to leave the property). Others shows included those spending millions to retrofit retired Atlas missile silos and thousands on security systems with customized software. Many episodes tended to focus on preppers with large rural properties where they can build and do whatever they want. Or they own property or a dwelling in the county or backwoods where they can bugout in an emergency. In an effort to maintain the shows high ratings, the show later seemed to focus on more and more extreme preppers wherein lies the problem and the reason for this book. Not everyone has the resources, skills, means or mental toughness to prep to extremes. Thus the concept of middle ground prepping was born.

Over the course of history it is now obvious that government led civil defense efforts in the U.S. were always one step behind and reactionary. In WWI citizens never thought a domestic attack was probable so they did not really plan or prepare for the possibility. Then the Japanese attacked the naval fleet at Pearl Harbor on December 7, 1941. While this was not yet technically U.S. soil, (Hawaii didn't become a state until August 21, 1959) our naval base operations had thousands of U.S. military personnel and citizens on the island. As a result, civil defense planning had to change to account for the possibility of additional domestic attacks.

In the early 80's, the possibility of a commercial nuclear reactor in the U.S having a catastrophic meltdown was said to be about the same as two 747 Jumbo jets colliding over Yankee Stadium in NY during a ball game. But no one really ever considered terrorists flying planes into the World Trade Center. Who thought that three decades later this country would be fighting religiously radicalized tribesman in the Middle East?

Summary

As stated, you can see that modern day prepping is a throw-back to the self-sufficiency of the Great Depression, sacrifices for our nation's war efforts and deep rooted religious beliefs. Most preppers today learned their skills from the Silent Generation and continue to hand down the practices to their children. Close to 86 million "Millennials" will now carry the prepping torch into the mid-21st century and the government will once again try and figure out how to keep them motivated to prepare for what comes next.

References:

1. Weems, John Edward. *Galveston Hurricane of 1900*, Handbook of Texas.
2. Kerr, Thomas J., *Civil Defense in the U.S.*, Westview Press (Boulder, CO): 1983. p12. ISBN 978-0-86531-586-0.

3. Green, Walter G., editor, *Council of National Defense and State Defense Councils*, Electronic Encyclopaedia of Civil Defense and Emergency Management. August 17, 2003.

4. Time Magazine, *The Younger Generation*, November 5, 1951 | Vol. LVIII No. 19.

5. Bruce Robinson (March 30, 2011), *The Blitz,*. BBC. Retrieved March 27, 2012.

6. Suburban Emergency Management Project, *SEMP Biot #243: What Is Civil Defense? World War I through the Eisenhower Administration*, August 1, 2005.

7. Civil Defense: The Truman Administration (Entry 0113) from *The Electronic Encyclopaedia of Civil Defense and Emergency Management* edited by Walter G. Green III.

8. David Greenberg, *Fallout Can Be Fun - How the Cold War civil-defense programs became farce*, www.Slate.com, February 20, 2003.

9. Bill Ganzel, the Ganzel Group, www.livinghistoryfarm.org, 2007.

10. Tennessee Emergency Management Agency, *History of Emergency Management*, http://www.co.mifflin.pa.us/.

11. FitzGerald, Frances (September 22, 1986), Rajneeshpuram, The New Yorker, retrieved July 12, 2011.

12. Flaccus, Gillian, *Ore. Town Never Recovered From Scare*, Associated Press, October 19, 2001.

13. Carus, W. Seth (2002), *Bioterrorism and Biocrimes* (PDF), The Minerva Group, Inc., ISBN 1-4101-0023-5.

14. USA Today staff, *Victims of the Oklahoma City bombing*, Associated Press, June 20, 2001, Archived from the original on February 27, 2011.

15. Shariat, Sheryll; Sue Mallonee; Shelli Stephens-Stidham, *Oklahoma City Bombing Injuries*, http://www.ok.gov/health2/documents/OKC_ Bombing.pdf, December 1998.

16. History.com staff, *Oklahoma City Bombing*, http://www.history.com/topics/oklahoma-city-bombing, 1995

17. Whitaker, Brian (21 August 2003). *Bomb type and tactics point to al-Qaida*. The Guardian (London: Guardian Media Group). Retrieved 11 July 2009.

18. History.com staff, *9/11 Attacks*, http://www.history.com/topics/9-11-attacks, 2010

19. Kotz, Deborah (April 24, 2013), *Injury toll from Marathon bombs reduced to 264*, The Boston Globe, Retrieved April 29, 2013.

20. Seelye, Katherine Q., *Bombing Suspect Cites Islamic Extremist Beliefs as Motive*, The New York Times. et al. Retrieved April 23, 2013.

21. President Thomas S. Monson, *That Noble Gift—Love at Home*, Church News, May 12, 2001, 7.

22. Church World Service, *Prepare to Care: A Guide to Disaster Ministry in Your*

Congregation, 9th Edition,
http://www.associatedchurches.org/clientimag
es/52868/missions/disaster%20ministry-
missions%20sect.%203.pdf, 2002,

23. Genzlinger, Neil (March 11, 2012), *Doomsday Has Its Day in the Sun,* The New York Times, Retrieved May 28, 2012.

24. Lactis, Erik (May 15, 2012), *Preppers do their best to be ready for the worst,* The Seattle Times, Retrieved October 25, 2013.

25. North, John (28 May 2012), *Doomsday Preppers' casting director aims to be prepared, too,* Asheville Daily Planet, Retrieved 18 November 2012.

Chapter 2 – The Government Can't Do It All

Based on personal experience as a Federal Emergency Management Agency (FEMA) – Community Emergency Response Team (CERT) and American Red Cross – Disaster Services instructor, our government cannot be totally responsible for our personal emergency preparedness. You should be able to see that for yourself simply by looking at FEMA responses to Hurricane Katrina and Sandy.

Hurricane Katrina

Hurricane Katrina was arguably the first major test of the new Department of Homeland Security after September 11. Within days of Katrina's August 29, 2005 landfall, public debate arose about the local, state, and federal governments' role in the preparations for and response to the storm. "There have been questions on who was in charge of the disaster and who had jurisdictional authority. According to many media outlets, as well as many politicians, the response to the disaster was inadequate in terms of leadership and response."[1]

Massive hurricane Katrina photographed from satellite

In addition to thousands of National Guard troops called to help, hundreds of firefighters volunteered to help rescue victims ahead of the storm. But many police, fire, and EMS organizations from outside the affected areas were reportedly hindered or otherwise slowed in their efforts to send help and assistance to the area because FEMA had these volunteers go to Atlanta for two days of training classes on topics including sexual harassment and the history of FEMA.[2] FEMA was also accused of deliberately slowing things down, in an effort to ensure that all assistance and relief workers were coordinated properly. For example

- Michael D. Brown, the head of FEMA, on August 29, urged all fire and emergency services departments not to respond to counties and states affected by Hurricane Katrina without being requested and lawfully dispatched by state and local authorities under mutual aid agreements and the Emergency Management Assistance Compact.[3]

- FEMA interfered in the Astor Hotel's plans to hire 10 buses to carry approximately 500 guests to higher ground. Federal officials commandeered the buses, and told the guests to join thousands of other evacuees at the Ernest N. Morial Convention Center.[4]

- FEMA officials turned away three Wal-Mart trailer trucks loaded with water, prevented the Coast Guard from delivering 1,000 gallons of diesel fuel, and cut the Jefferson Parish emergency communications line, leading the sheriff to restore it and post armed guards to protect it from FEMA.[3]

- Additionally, more than 50 civilian aircraft responding to separate requests for evacuations from hospitals and other agencies swarmed to the area a day after Katrina hit, but FEMA blocked their efforts. Aircraft operators complained that FEMA waved off a number of evacuation attempts, saying the rescuers were not authorized. "Many planes and helicopters simply sat idle," said Thomas Judge, president of the Association. of Air Medical Services.[5]

- Senator Mary Landrieu (D-Louisiana), was particularly critical of FEMA's efforts and said in part, "The U.S. Forest Service had water-tanker aircraft available to help douse the fires raging on our riverfront, but FEMA has yet to accept the aid. When Amtrak offered trains to evacuate significant numbers of victims—far more efficiently than buses— FEMA again dragged its feet. Offers of medicine, communications equipment and other desperately needed items continue to flow in, only to be ignored by the agency." [6]

Within the United States and as delineated in the National Response Plan, response and planning is first and foremost a local government responsibility. When local government exhausts its resources, it then requests specific additional resources from the county level. The request process proceeds similarly from the county to the state to the federal government as additional resource needs are identified. Many of the problems that arose developed from inadequate planning and back-up communications systems at various levels. One example of this is that the City of New Orleans attempted to manage the disaster from a hotel ballroom with inadequate back-up communications plans instead of a properly staffed Emergency Operations Center. [7] When phone service failed, they had difficulty communicating their specific needs to the state Emergency Operations Center in Baton Rouge.

Additionally, local disaster planners were criticized for failing to take the needs of people with disabilities into consideration. Transportation, communication and shelters did not make provision for people with mobility, cognitive, or communication disabilities.

Cases were reported of wheelchair users being left behind, no provision being made for guide dogs, and essential equipment or medication not made available. Disability advocacy organizations criticized local, state and federal emergency authorities for not including disabled people in their planning and consultation.[8]

Superstorm Sandy

Seven years later superstorm Sandy hit the east coast on October 29, 2012. The storm had twice the diameter of high wind from the eye of the hurricane than did Katrina, and 17% more total energy at landfall. But Sandy had less storm surge, deaths, rainfall, and property damage. Given the scathing criticisms after the Katrina debacle, FEMA needed to improve. The following information was pulled from FEMA's *Hurricane Sandy FEMA After-Action Report*.[9]

© Dan Callister / Rex Features

Superstorm Sandy destruction in New Jersey

In an effort to get out in front of this storm, over 900 FEMA personnel pre-deployed and were on the ground when Sandy made landfall. Key pre-landfall actions included

- establishing Incident Support Bases in Massachusetts and New Jersey, as well as five Federal Staging Areas in New York, to pre-position commodities, generators, and communications vehicles (pre-staged commodities included 892,000 liters of water, 561,000 meals, 11,900 blankets and cots, 183 generators, 30 infant and toddler kits, two Durable Medical Equipment [DME] kits, and two Consumable Medical Supplies [CMS] kits);
- deploying liaison officers (LNOs) and 13 Incident Management Assistance Teams (IMATs) to emergency operations centers in Connecticut, Delaware, the District of Columbia, Maine, Maryland, Massachusetts, New Jersey, New York, Pennsylvania, Rhode Island, Virginia, and Vermont;
- activating the National Response Coordination Center (NRCC)—the multiagency coordination center that coordinates overall Federal support for major disasters and emergencies—to a Level 1, its highest level, as well as activating all Emergency Support Functions (ESFs) and the Regional Response Coordination Centers (RRCCs) for FEMA Regions I, II, III, and IV;

- deploying nine National Urban Search and Rescue Task Forces, including eight with waterborne rescue capabilities;
- deploying all six Mobile Emergency Response System (MERS) detachments—which provide deployable, command, control, and incident communications capabilities—to 11 states across the East Coast;
- pre-staging 165 ground ambulances and associated medical teams; and
- deploying three Regional Disability Integration Specialists (RDISs) to coordinate with state and local partners and the disability community.

Additionally, to aid in the response effort, the President issued emergency declarations for 11 states before Sandy even made landfall. The day after landfall, the President issued disaster declarations for New York, New Jersey, and Connecticut.

While all this pre-planning helped significantly, 8.5 million customers were left without power, New York tunnels and subways were flooded and 9.3 million gallons of fuel needed to be trucked in just for emergency first responders in New York and New Jersey.

Additionally, the After Action Report identified several key areas of improvement:

- **Integrating Federal senior leader coordination and communications into response and recovery operations.** – This is not unusual since communication is the number one issue in almost every emergency situation. However, elected and appointed Federal senior leaders were deeply involved in coordinating Sandy response and recovery efforts. As Federal senior leaders worked aggressively to anticipate and address the needs of state, local, and tribal partners, these Federal partners did not always inform the National Response Coordination Center of independent actions taken to support response and recovery efforts. This caused miscommunication, delays, and often redundant efforts.

- **Coordinating Emergency Support Functions (ESF) and Recovery Support Functions (RSF) to support disaster response and recover.** - As an example, Sandy left 8.5 million customers without power and contributed to significant fuel shortages in parts of New York and New Jersey. FEMA senior leaders looked to ESF #12 (Energy) —coordinated by the U.S. Department of Energy (DOE) — to coordinate Federal efforts related to energy restoration. DOE struggled to meet this requirement and lacked the operational capability to fully engage supporting Federal departments and energy-sector partners in addressing energy-restoration challenges.

- **Refining the mission assignment process.** – Mission assignments are work orders that FEMA issues to other Federal departments or agencies, directing completion of a specified task by those departments or agencies. These assignments must be in place in order for FEMA to reimburse Federal departments or agencies for performing disaster-related activities. Although a simple task, approximately 40 percent of mission assignments from October 26 to November 20 took longer than one day to process in order to correct errors and clarify specific mission requirements, thereby delaying completion of tasks.

- **Implementing incident management structures.** – FEMA chose to use a combined functional and geographic approach management structure for the response and initial recovery activities in New York and New Jersey. While lauded as a good choice for such an event, issues arose when local (geographical) and functional representatives could not agree (or be willing to relinquish control) on certain issues.

Without a return of responsibility to the states, the federalization of routine disasters will continue to require FEMA to become involved with a new disaster somewhere in the United States at the current pace of every 2.5 days. This high operational tempo is affecting FEMA's overall preparedness because it keeps FEMA perpetually in a response mode, leaving little time and few resources for catastrophic preparedness. Hurricane Sandy illustrated this problem once again. [10]

Do Americans Really Want the Government Spending Our Money?

Given the history of our government agency mismanagement, do Americans really want to pay the federal government to handle our nation's emergency planning and response efforts? According to the Government Accountability Office, federal agencies "set a new record for improper payments in 2014, shelling out $125 billion in questionable benefits. While the errors were spread among 22 federal agencies, three programs stood out: Medicare, Medicaid and the Earned Income Tax Credit. Together, the three programs accounted for more than $93 billion in improper payments."[11] "This taxpayer money was not spent securing our borders, it was not spent on national defense, and it was not spent contributing to a safety net for those in need," said Sen. Ron Johnson, R-Wis., chairman of the Senate Committee on Homeland Security and Governmental Affairs.

FEMA local disaster operations center

Recent cover stories have either shattered our confidence in, or bolstered our impression of several federal agencies:

- **FEMA** – "FEMA spent $878.8 million on nearly 25,000 manufactured homes that the agency is paying to store around the country largely because its own regulations prohibited placing the homes in flood plains, such as New Orleans."[12]

- **Social Security** - At least 6.5 million active Social Security numbers belong to people who are at least 112 years old and likely deceased. Only 35 living individuals worldwide had reached that age as of October 2013, according to the Gerontology Research Group. On the good side, the IRS estimates it prevented $24.2 billion in fraudulent identity theft refunds in 2013. Still, the IRS actually paid out $5.8 billion in fraudulent refunds that it realized were fraudulent only later. [13]

- **Veteran's Affairs** - Despite the fact that multiple VA Inspector General reports have linked many VA patient care problems to widespread mismanagement within VA facilities and GAO findings that VA bonus pay has no clear link to performance, the department has consistently defended its celebration of executives who presided over these events, while giving them glowing performance reviews and cash bonuses of up to $63,000.[14]

- **IRS** - On May 14, 2013, the Treasury Inspector General for Taxpayer Administration released a report detailing an audit of IRS activities and confirmed that, "the IRS used inappropriate criteria to identify organizations applying for tax-exempt status." The audit confirms that targeting of conservative groups began in 2010. The report also confirms that, despite repeated denials to the contrary, IRS officials had knowledge of such activities as early as 2011.[15]

- **USAID** - U.S. Agency for International Development was the lead agency for the overall U.S. response to the Ebola epidemic in West Africa, partnering with CDC, which was the medical lead. The United States has spent $1.4 billion on its Ebola mission in West Africa, with most of it going to Liberia. Deploying the military cost $360 million, not including the construction, staffing, and operating expenses at treatment centers built. Only 28 Ebola patients were treated at the 11 treatment units built by the U.S. military, American officials now say.[16] That is a cost of $5 million per patient!

At the time of Hurricane Katrina, FEMA relied on manual processes, such as spreadsheets, to carry out their mission. But following Katrina, Congress passed the Post-Katrina Emergency Management Reform Act of 2006, which required FEMA to implement a state-of-the-art logistics management system that would allow a real-time visibility of items at each point throughout the logistics system.[17]

To comply with the Act, over the past nine years FEMA has worked to implement its new Logistics Supply Chain Management System (LSCMS). The LSCMS program, based on commercially available software, is intended to provide greater quality control by automating FEMA's internal processes and to integrate FEMA's partners' systems, giving FEMA a platform to track supplies from partners. FEMA's partners include other federal agencies; non-governmental organizations; state, local, and tribal governments; and the private sector.[17]

However, the Inspector General's recent report found that LCSMS falls short of the performance, schedule, and cost requirements that were set out at the time LCSMS was created. The program is delayed by at least 19 months, and FEMA estimates that the system will ultimately cost $231 million more than originally estimated. Further, the current LCSMS does not interface with FEMA's partners' systems and does not allow real-time visibility into FEMA's supply chain system.[17]

Unlike welfare, food stamp programs and unemployment benefits; there are NO federal government programs designed to "push" emergency preparedness funds to Americans that need help preparing. There are NO tax incentives to "write-off" preparedness expenses, like emergency food and water supplies. There are, however, several programs designed to make Americans more aware of the need to prepare, but no funding is currently available to reimburse such an effort (e.g., the Community Emergency Response Team program). In the past, some state level agencies have received federal grant funding that allowed them to indirectly procure basic emergency kits for those underprivileged and low income persons who otherwise could not afford them. However, many of these kits were ultimately given out to emergency volunteers.

Currently, FEMA only provides state and local governments with preparedness program funding in the form of Non-Disaster Grants to "enhance the capacity of state and local emergency responders to prevent, respond to, and recover from a weapons of mass destruction terrorism incident involving chemical, biological, radiological, nuclear, and explosive devices and cyber-attacks."[18] This does not apply to natural disaster preparedness specifically, but theoretically these capacities could be used in such cases.

As citizens have witnessed during some of our country's most horrific natural and man-made disasters, everyone pitches in during a crisis. FEMA has been attempting to formalize this phenomenon for years with both the Citizens Corps and the CERT programs. The most effective community preparedness occurs at all levels including

- local government,
- public and private sectors,
- neighborhoods, and
- individuals and families.

Local Government

The "local government" that we speak of regarding emergency preparedness generally consists of the following local city, county and statewide government agencies:

- Emergency Management,
- Law Enforcement,
- Fire and Rescue,
- Emergency Medical Services (often provided by Fire and Rescue),
- Public Works, and
- Health & Human Services.

Not every locality will have all of these agencies. Cities generally reside within a county and often times the Emergency Management and Health & Human Services agencies will oversee such activities for cities within their jurisdiction. Each city however, may have police and fire departments.

In terms of emergency preparedness planning, these agencies have the responsibility to

- develop, exercise, and improve emergency operations plans;
- ensure first responders have the necessary skills and resources to protect and serve the community;
- get community comment in the planning process;
- provide accurate and dependable information; and
- support additional training, practice skills, and manage volunteer programs.

As mentioned above, a good deal of the actual training, resources, and emergency exercises are funded by both state and federal grants.

One thing many local governments worked on in the post 9/11 era was holding community "Emergency Fairs." However, only those entities with leaders who had a passion for preparedness really promoted the public fair concept. As Peter Drucker said, "Whenever anything is being accomplished, it is being done, I have learned, by a monomaniac with a mission."

These emergency fairs were designed as family friendly half to full day events to share preparedness information with the public and meet local fire, police and other emergency personnel. Emergency vendors were invited to showcase their emergency supplies.

Local utility companies also attended to discuss how they handle emergencies.

All emergency fairs tried to provide some worthwhile "give-away" to attract attendees. It could have been a first aid kit, a small single person emergency kit or something similar. Each vendor attending was encouraged to provide a "door prize" as well to further entice the community to attend.

Having coordinated and supported (as a vendor) many such events the attendees showed up for the free gift and paid little attention to the valuable information available at the fair. Without the lure of something free, the public is just not that interested in what their community leaders are doing to prepare for local disasters. There is this implicit trust that our leaders will take care of everything.

Local government websites also went through a metamorphosis in the post 9/11 era to include pages dedicated to emergency preparedness and specific local disaster information. Many such pages were difficult to find and consisted of enormous lists of other websites where information could be had. Little updating has been done to many of these pages and they languish in the dark corners of the Internet.

Public and Private-Sectors

Both public and private sector companies have a central role in our community preparedness plans since they are responsible for a good deal of the infrastructure and supplies that we depend on every day. This would include companies that provide telephone, radio, television, transportation, and banking services as well as food, medicines, health care, insurance and recovery supplies. This sector also includes non-government organizations (NGOs) such as voluntary organizations and faith-based organizations that act as partners in responding to local and statewide disasters. Such organizations typically provide temporary shelter, emergency food, counseling services, pet rescue, and assistance with special needs persons.[10]

Many public and private companies have contractual relationships with local governments to provide goods or services at pre-determined rates for disaster relief including

- Local building supply stores providing large quantities of plywood and other building materials.
- Rental companies providing portable toilets, generators, and heavy equipment for debris removal.
- Office supply stores providing copy services and stationary supplies.
- Local restaurants providing food for first responders and volunteers.
- Safety supply companies providing flares, traffic cones, and delimiters.

Then there are the primary infrastructure companies who are the only ones who can fix and repair services and transportation routes disrupted by a disaster. These paid service providers would include

- Electric utilities that have the trained manpower and equipment to repair downed power lines and damaged electrical grid components.
- Gas utilities that can repair damaged distribution pipelines and re-light pilot lights in homes.
- Communication companies that can repair phone, cable and Internet lines and rebuild damaged cell towers.
- Construction companies that have the equipment to repair damaged roadways to ensure commerce and disaster supplies continue to flow.

Along with local government, many such companies also felt the need to hold emergency fairs in their building or on campus to show good community leadership and a real interest in their employees. As in the public fairs, employees wandered around the vendor area looking for free items during work hours. During lunch the attendees would leave to fully capture their allotted lunch time, only to return back during work hours. The message being, people are willing to waste some work time to get free preparedness stuff but not their personal time.

Buddhist Tzu Chi Foundation volunteers assist with fire preparedness

The NGOs, which are mostly voluntary organizations and faith-based organizations, can offer significant support during and after a disaster. Prominent and well known NGOs include

- The American Red Cross,
- The Salvation Army,
- Southern Baptist Disaster Relief,
- Buddhist Tzu Chi Foundation,
- United Methodist Committee on Relief,
- Adventist Community Services,
- Brethren Disaster Ministries,
- Catholic Charities USA Disaster Response,
- Children's Disaster Services,
- Lutheran Disaster Response,
- Presbyterian Disaster Assistance,
- Volunteers of America,

- Americorps, and
- National Animal Rescue and Sheltering Coalition.

There are hundreds more NGOs large and small that plan for, train volunteers, and support disasters of all types around the country. Most have a specific niche in which they provide services and goods to victims of disasters.

The key to being a viable NGO is to be fully embedded in the local, state or national emergency planning process. Then it takes constant training with professional responders and local government agencies to earn their respect. Once the local government understands the capabilities and limitations of an NGO, both organizations can begin to emphasize their strengths. The last thing that local (or federal) government agencies need is to actively manage an NGO in the middle of a crisis. The NGOs must be trusted to provide their niche service or goods directly to disaster victims with little management and disruption to other disaster relief operations.

However, local governments understand all too well that many issues can arise with NGOs that make dependence upon them uncertain. These can include

- lack of funds,
- poor governance,
- absence of strategic planning,
- poor networking,
- poor communication,

- limited capacity,
- inability to retain volunteers,
- political interference, and
- relationships with international NGOs.

Like any other endeavor, the success of most NGOs is fully dependent upon the interest, passion and dedication of the leadership. When leadership changes and the passion fades so does the effectiveness of the organization. Often times the NGO forget they are a supporting member of a larger disaster relief effort. The successful NGOs are those that provide honest assistance to those in need efficiently and with compassion.

Neighborhoods

The term "neighborhood" can mean any local area and can be as small as the households adjacent to yours, your street, or your living area (e.g., apartment/condo complex, residential community, etc.). The fundamental key to neighborhood preparedness is knowing your neighbor's needs and capabilities and sharing the same about yourself. Perhaps they have an elderly parent living with them that may be alone during the day and need additional time evacuating, or a dog in the backyard that must be fed. Can a stay-at-home parent be available to pick up your children from school in an emergency? Is there a nurse or doctor living in the neighborhood in case you can't get to a hospital for a medical emergency?

It is also a good idea to become familiar with local first responders that service your neighborhood. Do you all know where your closest fire station is? Are you familiar with community alerts and warnings (e.g., tornado sirens, creek and river flood statuses, etc.), potential evacuation routes, and how best to get critical information? The National Night Out program is an excellent way to invite first responders into your neighborhood to meet the community and introduce children to the safety of first responders. The biggest problem is that National Night Out happens only once a year in early August.

Unfortunately for many of us, meeting your neighbors (outside of the few adjacent to your home) only occurs when there is an emergency. Hectic lives lead most of us to an occasional wave of the hand to neighbors but rarely allows us to sit down and "get to know" our neighbors.

Neighborhood Watch groups are a good way of meeting your neighbors and protecting your neighborhood at the same time. Launched in 1972, Neighborhood Watch counts on citizens to organize themselves and work with law enforcement to keep a trained eye and ear on their communities, while demonstrating their presence at all times of day and night. Neighborhood Watch works because it reduces opportunities for crime to occur; it doesn't rely on altering or changing the criminal's behavior or motivation.[19]

As in most things, such groups are formed when an individual seizes on the idea and pushes the development process. As the neighborhood evolves and babies are born, families drift apart again, so the

Neighborhood Watch group languishes and all lose interest. Such groups need to remain active and informative for the neighborhood in order to provide any protection. While you may see Neighborhood Watch signs still posted in a neighborhood, odds are high that there are no ongoing activities or meetings. This is typical in the death of a Neighborhood Watch program.

However, today many neighborhoods/communities have Facebook pages where residents can keep up with neighborhood events and happenings. Information about lost dogs, suspicious vehicles, loud parties, road repairs, and special events are often transmitted real time via the Internet. While this does provide a needed service of information, it still does little to build personal relationships which are critical to effectively helping others in an emergency.

Individuals and Family

In today's world, individuals and families have the responsibility to

- eliminate and reduce hazards at their homes, which can minimize the overall effect of a disaster;
- turn off their utilities if needed;
- develop an emergency plan;
- get emergency kits for home, cars and work;
- develop an emergency communication plan including emergency meeting places;
- monitor the Emergency Alert System (EAS) during critical events; and

- understand emergency plans at their workplaces and children's schools.

According to FEMA, you may need to survive on your own after a disaster. This means having your own food, water, and other supplies in sufficient quantity to last for at least three days. Local officials and relief workers will be on the scene after a disaster, but they cannot reach everyone immediately. You could get help in hours, or it might take days.[20]

Nothing can be more detrimental to the response to a catastrophe than if first responders must waste vital time and resources taking care of those who could have taken care of themselves. Every community has individuals who collectively form a sizable vulnerable population. Typically, the vulnerable population consists of the mentally and physically disabled, the elderly, non-English-speaking immigrants, and children. As was demonstrated during Hurricane Katrina and Superstorm Sandy, a society fails when it fails those most in need.[10]

So, the concept of individuals helping in emergencies is first to take care of yourself and your family. Next, see if neighbors can use your assistance. Once your neighbors are considered safe and cared for, then, and only then, should individuals consider volunteering in a larger capacity.

However, as the 9/11 Commission noted, "The 'first' first responders on 9/11, as in most catastrophes, were private-sector civilians. Because 85 percent of our nation's critical infrastructure is controlled not by government but by the private sector, private-sector civilians are likely to be the first responders in any future catastrophes."[21]

Summary

Despite all the government's efforts to get citizens to prepare, recent data suggests Americans are far from becoming a nation of prepared citizens:[22]

- 46.1% have no evacuation kit,
- 65.1% have no communication plan, and
- 60.6% have no emergency meeting place.

Emergency preparedness is considered a hobby by many and is an excellent opportunity to promote family communication and responsibility. If you are committed to preparing you and your family for emergencies consider

- reading about the best ways to prepare for various disasters common in your area;
- taking training classes in preparedness, first aid, and disaster response skills (contact your local fire department for upcoming community emergency response team classes;
- practicing skills and emergency plans periodically with all family members;
- reporting suspicious activity to authorities; and
- volunteering with an established organization known to local government agencies.

References:

1. Nancy Pelosi (February 8, 2006). *Katrina Response a Scandal of Incompetence and Cronyism*, California Chronicle. Retrieved 26 September 2010. [Dead link].
2. Firefighters stuck in Ga. awaiting orders, Greg Bluestein, Associated Press Writer. USA Today. September 7, 2005.
3. Shane, Scott, *After Failures, Government Officials Play Blame Game*, New York Times, September 5, 2005
4. Staff Writer, *Katrina at a glance*, WKMG-TV. September 1, 2005. [Dead link]
5. Patrick Stuver (2005), *Maximizing Emergency Communication*, Risk and Insurance Management, Retrieved 2008-04-18. [Dead link]
6. Landrieu, Mary, *U.S. Senator Mary Landrieu, D-La. (press release)*, Senator Landrieu's Website, September 3, 2005. Retrieved on July 15, 2006. [Dead link]
7. Lynn E. Delisi, *The Katrina disaster and its lessons*, World Psychiatry, 2006 February; 5(1): 3–4.
8. Tady, Megan. *Disabled People 'Left Behind' in Emergency Planning - The NewStandard*, Newstandardnews.net, Retrieved 2013-05-21.
9. FEMA, *Hurricane Sandy FEMA After-Action Report*, July 1, 2013.
10. Steven P. Bucci, Ph.D., David Inserra, Jonathan Lesser, Ph.D., Matt A. Mayer, Brian Slattery, Jack Spencer and Katie Tubb, *After Hurricane Sandy: Time to Learn and Implement the Lessons in Preparedness,*

Response, and Resilience, The Heritage Foundation, http://www.heritage.org/research/reports/2013/10/after-hurricane-sandy-time-to-learn-and-implement-the-lessons. Retrieved March 16, 2015.

11. Stephen Ohlemacher, *Improper payments by federal agencies reach a record $125B*, Yahoo News, http://news.yahoo.com/improper-payments-federal-agencies-reach-record-125b-071024080--politics.html. Retrieved March 17, 2015.

12. Mimi Hall, USA Today, *Senators hear 'shocking examples' of FEMA waste*, Posted 2/13/2006. Retrieved March 17, 2015.

13. United States Government Accountability Office, *Report to Congressional Requesters, IDENTITY THEFT AND TAX FRAUD - Enhanced Authentication Could Combat Refund Fraud, but IRS Lacks an Estimate of Costs, Benefits and Risks*, January 2015.

14. House Committee on Veterans' Affairs, *VA Accountability Watch*, https://veterans.house.gov/accountability. Retrieved March 17, 2015.

15. Committee on Ways and Means, *The IRS Political Discrimination Investigation*, https://waysandmeans.house.gov/forms/form/?ID=2538. Retrieved March 17, 2015.

16. Norimitsu Onishi, *Empty Ebola Clinics in Liberia Are Seen as Misstep in U.S. Relief Effort*, The New York Times, April 11, 2015.

17. Marika Mikuriya, *Audit Says FEMA Still Not Ready to Deliver Supplies During Emergencies*, RegBlog (December 1, 2014). Retrieved from http://www.regblog.org/2014/12/01/mikuriya-fema-disaster-preparedness/.

18. FEMA, Preparedness (Non-Disaster) Grants, https://www.fema.gov/preparedness-non-disaster-grants.

19. National Crime Prevention Council, http://www.ncpc.org/topics/home-and-neighborhood-safety/neighborhood-watch, Retrieved April 8, 2015.

20. FEMA, *Are You Ready? – An In-depth Guide to Citizen Preparedness*, http://www.fema.gov/pdf/areyouready/areyour eady_full.pdf, Retrieved April 8, 2015.

21. National Commission on Terrorist Attacks Upon the United States, *Final Report of the National Commission on Terrorist Attacks Upon the United States,* (New York: W.W. Norton & Company, 2004), p. 317.

22. Governing.com, The American Housing Survey, conducted by the Census Bureau and U.S. Department of Housing and Urban Development, 2013, http://www.governing.com/gov-data/safety-justice/emergency-preparedness-metro-areas-household-survey-data.html, Retrieved April 2, 2015.

Chapter 3 – Disaster Awareness

There are serious considerations when starting your emergency preparations and the least of which is trying to understand the various phases of a disaster. Even more complicated is trying to understand the different psychological stages of disaster recovery. To start, let's examine the four phases of every disaster.

Four Phases of Disaster

There are generally four physical phases that are associated with all disasters:

- preparedness phase,
- situational awareness phase,
- impact phase, and
- aftermath phase.

Preparedness phase (or minimizing risk) – Think of the preparedness phase as the time you have to consider whether or not you want to buy some type of insurance to minimize a risk that is coming such as an earthquake or a flood. Either you are convinced that a disaster will, at some point, impact your life, or you are not. The former will use the preparedness phase to collect those items to help them weather the storm and minimize their discomfort during the disaster. The latter will be on the 5 o'clock news saying "I never thought something like this would ever happen here."

If you are serious about preparing yourself and your family to minimize the disruption to your way of life and your relative comfort, start with the basics. First and foremost you will need water. More is ALWAYS better when it comes to water. Besides drinking it, you may use water for cooking, hand and body hygiene, and providing first aid. Food is next and any food is better than no food. Try to avoid thirst provoking foods; remember many canned foods may be high in sodium and thus induce thirst. Having a good variety of foods will be an advantage in terms of appetite and health too.

Then consider your shelter needs. If your home is habitable (which it may not be after an earthquake or tornado), stay there. If not, you will need a backup shelter, such as a tent, to camp out in your backyard if the area is safe to do so. Sanitation is probably the least remembered function of your emergency supplies, but without water to flush toilets, you will need a portable toilet of some sort. First aid supplies are necessary to minimize infection and the debilitating results of an injury. You will need emergency lighting which now has many options, from light sticks to flashlights to lanterns. Many of these devices do not require batteries which eliminates the need to keep fresh batteries in stock. Finally, make sure you have some means (cell phone, radio or TV powered without electricity) of listening to the Emergency Alert System (EAS) to understand the situation you are in and how to get additional help if needed. This will be discussed in more depth in Chapter 5.

Given the disaster and specific situation, the order of your preparations may change. For example, if you can no longer stay in your home and must be outside but it is raining, shelter may be priority number one. Having all this "stuff" is great, but you really should practice using it to ensure it will meet your needs during an emergency. Perhaps have the family rely solely on your emergency supplies for one day or even a weekend. This will provide valuable lessons and identify areas of preparation where you need to improve. Remember to restock your supplies after the exercise.

Next, you will need well thought out emergency plans (preferably written down) that must consider all the possible emergency/disaster scenarios that you could reasonably expect in your geographic area. While considering the plan for each unique scenario, consider the Impact and Aftermath phases discussed herein.

Finally, ensure that you have a family communication plan with several redundant layers (e.g., voice, text, physical meeting place) to ensure that you can either make contact with your family members or meet them in the Aftermath phase.

Situational awareness phase (or where are you?) – It never ceases to amaze me how many folks will admit after a disaster on the 5 o'clock news that "I had no idea this was coming." Understanding your current location and the issue at hand is situational awareness and will do wonders for helping you survive a disaster or emergency event.

Living here in northern California, our weather rarely reaches extremes. There is rain, hail, wind and thunderstorms, but nothing like Seattle, Houston, Tacoma or Kansas City. Yet, it is still important to understand what the weather is for the next 7 days! Why? It may be critical to

- know how to prepare livestock and property for the impending weather,
- ensure your backup generator is fueled and operable,
- secure any loose objects around the house and double-check the supports on young trees, and
- check the fuel in vehicles and the backup fuel supply.

By doing so, nothing is a surprise and you are prepared.

With the rare exception of earthquakes, most severe weather can be seen coming and is forecast by local meteorologists. As the weather gets closer, local TV and radio stations will start announcing weather "Watches" and "Warnings." Do NOT discount these reports! Although we have a good idea of what is coming, the actual severity of the weather is often not well-known and could surprise you.

"Where were you at 4 PM today?" is one of the questions asked during emergency preparedness presentations. Without fail, there are usually always three responses, "At work, at home, or driving." These are the places where you need to be prepared! If you are driving to visit friends or relatives, have you checked the weather forecasts along your route?

If there is snow possible, do you have chains and cold weather clothing? What if you get lost (the opposite of situational awareness) and are forced to stay in your vehicle for an extended period?

Knowing where you are in the world, what your surroundings are, who is around you, and how you would react to an emergency, are the hallmarks of prudent situational awareness. For example, if you are shopping at the mall, are you on the first or second floor? Are you at the far end of the mall away from where you parked your car, or are you near your car? Having this knowledge in the front of your mind could make the difference between saving your life, or not, in an emergency. If you have not thought of how to get out of the burning plane or hotel, escape the shooter at the mall, or get rescued from a remote car accident before it happens, you are behind the curve.

In the words of Louis Pasteur, "Did you ever observe to whom the accidents happen? Chance favors only the prepared mind." So, practice your situational awareness and get in touch with your surroundings.

Impact phase (or - it hits the fan) – The impact phase is where the disaster occurs and your preparedness efforts and situational awareness pays off.

Tornado damage in Oklahoma

The actual disaster can be terrifying to the unprepared and can result in their inability to act and help themselves or make good decisions. It is this group that can only hope for assistance in the aftermath phase of a disaster. The reality is the majority of those affected by a disaster fall into this category. This phase can vary from the slow, low-threat buildup associated with some types of floods to the violent, dangerous, and destructive outcomes associated with earthquakes, tornadoes, and explosions.

Based upon your preparations and situational awareness planning, you should have a fairly realistic impression of the outcome of the disaster. This means those that are more prepared and have planned for such a disaster most likely will find themselves less traumatized by the event. Executing your emergency plans should allow you to endure the event without thinking, "Am I going to die?" Key actions during the impact phase include

- not getting injured,
- executing your emergency plan,
- adapting to changing situations, and
- making good survival decisions.

All of which should have been considered previously in the preparedness phase.

While your entire family may not be together during the impact phase, you should take comfort in knowing that all family members have been trained for such an event. Certainly you will be concerned for them and based upon your family communication plan, you know that you can ultimately make contact with them since you are all following the same plan.

Aftermath phase (or what now?) – One of the first activities provided by first responders in the aftermath of a disaster is rescue operations. However, do not assume that you are going to be at the top of the rescue list because you think you are special! Just as in disaster medical operations, search and rescue (SAR) operations will also prioritize the need for SAR operations. You should expect that the elderly, hospitalized, mentally ill, handicapped, the very young, and those still in harm's way may get priority rescue support. SAR priorities are generally geared toward rescuing the "low-hanging fruit" first; that is, those most easily rescued are rescued first. This allows the rescue teams to do the most good for the greatest number of people. Your preparedness efforts should hold you until SAR teams can get to you, but be patient and understand that others may need help more than you do.

Depending upon the type, severity, and duration of the event; there will be near-term and long-term decisions you will need to make. For example, near-term decisions will include activating your event specific emergency plan for your immediate water, food, and shelter needs. Longer-term decisions may include

- how to get back to work (given fuel shortages) or finding new work if your company was severely impacted by the event,
- contacting your insurance provider(s) for relief,
- applying for FEMA aid,
- securing temporary living quarters until your home is reconstructed or relocated, and
- restocking your emergency supplies.

Again, during this phase of a disaster, it is critical that you maintain your hygiene habits and prevent injuries as medical aid may be difficult to come by after a large-scale event. Carefully evaluate all your activities to ensure you do not

- over-expose yourself to cold or heat,
- put yourself in dangerous situations that could result in severe injuries, or
- expose yourself to large groups of people or areas that could be breeding grounds for unwanted diseases.

While helping your fellow-man, who may not have prepared as well as you, is admirable, ensure that such actions do not compromise your family's critical supplies. After all, the object of preparing is to have you and your family survive with minimal disruption to your lives. Which leads us to potential security issues as the Aftermath phase draws out. Again, depending upon the severity and extent of the disaster, it is not outside the realm of possibility to have widespread looting and roving gangs looking for food. How will you protect your supplies?

Regardless of the severity of a disaster, whether local, regional or statewide; your outcome will be dependent upon the 4 phases identified herein. While many of these topics are not necessarily pleasant to consider; doing so, could save your life or at least make it more comfortable in the event of a severe disaster. The world is seeing more and more severe weather in locations unaccustomed to such weather. Therefore, it is a disservice to your fellow-man NOT to do some preparedness planning! Because the more prepared people there are, the lesser the overall effect of the disaster. Yes, this does take some level of commitment to put such plans in place, but the alternative is even grimmer.

In Your Head

Now that the disaster has occurred, what can you expect from yourself in terms of emotions during the various psychological stages of disaster recovery? Depending upon which references you site, there can be anywhere from 3 to 7 stages of psychological disaster recovery. However, for the most part, there is general agreement that there are four main stages including

- heroic or rescue,
- honeymoon or remedy,
- disillusionment, and
- recovery or reconstruction.

Citizens helping others after Nepal Earthquake 2015

Heroic (or rescue) stage – Occurring at the time of the impact phase and in the immediate aftermath phase, the Heroic (or rescue) stage is characterized by shell-shocked citizens with emergency needs for food, water, and shelter. Feelings of grief and loss are strong at this stage, but so, too, are emotions of selfless concern for the well-being of others. There is a sense of the heroic, of people responding from the highest, most sublime part of themselves to help fellow human beings by rescuing, offering needed supplies, and generally giving the best of themselves to meet dire needs.[1]

The firemen who went up into the stricken Twin Towers after the 9/11 attacks in New York, thereby endangering and sometimes losing their own lives, are a good example of heroic stage. The heroic Search and Rescue teams that responded to Hurricane Katrina (2005) and the New Zealand earthquakes of 2010 and 2011are also examples. Individuals toiled long hours to rescue and assist survivors even though their own homes had been demolished in the disasters.

Honeymoon (or remedy) stage – From a few days after the disaster to about three to six months onward (depending on the disaster), a community tends to be in the honeymoon phase. Survivors – and their loved ones – feel relief at survival, and often there is still an emotional high of "I survived. That is what matters. The rest we can deal with." There is a strong sense in the community of having shared a terrible experience and lived through it. After the Boston Marathon bombings, Beantown rallied around the mantra "Boston Strong."

Public officials are often praised for their role in saving lives and organizing relief efforts. For agencies such as the Red Cross, this is an excellent opportunity for fundraising. This is because people open their wallets with relative generosity as a result of feeling moved by the intense media coverage of widespread suffering and touching tales of rescue and survival. Survivors experience high expectations about the help that they will get from official and governmental agencies towards rebuilding their lives: partly because many promises are made to them at this stage.[1]

Disillusionment stage – Inevitably, reality sets in. Governments put conditions on the assistance they will give, insurance companies find reasons not to pay out on survivors' once greatest asset – their home, and the media and some helping agencies leave the scene. This phase can last from several months to up to two years. No longer the focus of the world's (or even the region's) attention, survivors begin to experience a strong sense of anger, resentment, bitterness, and deep disappointment if they now begin to experience delays, failures, and/or unfulfilled hopes or promises of aid. People are exhausted by now, worn by the extreme stress of ongoing recovery effort.[1]

At this stage, survivors question aid and governmental agencies' promises, intentions, service delivery, and achievements. The grim reality of just how long and difficult a road it will be back to "normal" presents itself. People concentrate on rebuilding their own individual lives and solving individual problems. The feeling of "shared community" is lost.

Recovery (or reconstruction) stage – Lasting for several years following the disaster, this is the long-term phase of disaster recovery. It may proceed at a glacial pace and is probably not supremely interesting to the media (until anniversary days of the event, when follow-up media reports are prepared). The emotions that appear here can vary widely according to

- the status (emotional and financial) of survivors,
- the manner in which previous stages were handled, and
- the actual level of resources that have become available.

Survivors realize that they are ultimately responsible for solving the problems of their lives. If recovery efforts are visible, the community – and through that the individuals in it – achieve a sense of being empowered that fuels further recovery. If community efforts towards recovery are not visible, individuals are more at risk for succumbing to PTSD and other serious mental and physical un-wellness.[1]

After the Aftermath

Disasters, whether they are natural or man-made in origin, or contain elements of both, can cause extensive destruction, injury, and death. Regardless, profound mental health consequences to victims and first responders can be expected as a result of major disasters of all types. Additionally, technological advances are bringing disturbing up-close on-scene media coverage of disasters to more people than ever. Based on empirical study of disasters, the following main principles of disaster mental health have been established and described in the disaster mental health literature.[2]

1. **People are resilient**. - In efforts to identify mental health problems to be addressed, it is easy to overlook the resilience of the majority who do not develop psychiatric disorders, even after exposure to severe disaster trauma. Some people may even experience personal growth or have other positive outcomes.

2. **Psychiatric illnesses rare, emotional distress** – It should be fairly obvious that emotional distress after exposure to disasters is a normal response. Recurring dreams and hyperarousal (a state of increased psychological and physiological tension marked by such effects as reduced pain tolerance, anxiety, exaggeration of startle responses, insomnia, fatigue, and accentuation of personality traits) are particularly common manifestations of emotional responses to disasters.

3. **Not all survivor stress is the same** - Emotional distress is not posttraumatic stress disorder (PTSD). PTSD or any other psychiatric disorder is never normal, even if it occurs in relation to a disaster.

4. **Diagnose and treat psychiatric disorders due to disasters** - Psychiatric disorders developing in the wake of disasters deserve formal assessment and treatment just as in other settings. Accurate diagnosis is essential, because it determines the most appropriate type of intervention.

5. **PTSD is common post disaster** - PTSD usually develops quickly after disaster exposure (within the first few months), and it is often chronic, lasting many months to years. People who are not exposed to trauma - by physical endangerment; directly witnessing others being endangered, injured, or killed; or by having a close associate who was exposed - cannot be candidates for PTSD.

6. **Alcohol and drug abuse not normal after disasters**. - Although alcohol and drug use may increase in some groups after certain disasters, this occurrence does not regularly translate into new substance use disorders.

Mentally Prepare for an Emergency

Disasters, whether they are natural or man-made in origin, or contain elements of both, can cause extensive destruction, injury, and death. Regardless, profound mental health consequences to victims and first responders can be expected as a result of major disasters of all types.

Disorder caused by disasters disrupts the way we think and feel. Have you thought about how you can prepare yourself for the mental and emotional challenges of a disaster? Here are some tips about what to expect and how to make you more resilient for mental and emotional challenges before, during, and after a disaster.

Emergency planning - Actions you take for personal preparedness will improve your mental readiness for disasters. Because stress and fear from disasters make it hard for your brain to plan and make decisions, it is good to have written emergency plans and emergency kits available. Having family plans and emergency kits on hand also reassures your brain that you have resources to manage the event. Regaining some sense of control during an emergency, like knowing how to communicate and bring your family back together, will soothe a lot of stress you feel.

Training - Take a CPR course, first aid or Community Emergency Response Training class in order to better take care of yourself and family. Practice escape routes from your home in case of a fire with regularly scheduled fire drills. Practice your evacuation plan by loading up the car and heading to your pre-determined bug-out location.

Physical – Physical preparedness will get and keep you in good physical shape which will help your mental outlook and stress levels. Exercise itself is a great way to cope with stress and stimulate endorphin production to increase feelings of well-being and control. Stress and fear send hormones to your body that need to be purged in order to relax after a stressful event. Healthy eating, plenty of water (and less caffeine), plenty of rest and regular exercise will help your body rebalance those hormone levels and ease feelings of anxiety.

Simplification - Simplifying your life can significantly lower your stress levels. This can be accomplished by reducing material goods and having less stuff to maintain on a regular basis. Do you really need an RV, motorcycle, classic car and four bicycles? You can also clean up your finances by eliminating debt. Finally, take a good hard look at what are the most important things in your life. Spend your money on things that will simplify your life first and make it a better life. For example, if you spend hours a week watering your plants, install a drip system to do it automatically (unless you love watering those plants), or if you love spending time at home on the patio, make sure your patio furniture makes you feel comfortable.

Awareness – Be more aware of your emotions and don't suppress emotions because they are important messages from your body. If you are feeling anxious, there is a reason. Instead, work on tolerating difficult emotions without automatically over-reacting. This could help you manage stressful emotions caused by disasters.

Spirituality – Whether you regularly attend some religious event or not, spirituality is about understanding yourself and what makes you the way you are. Spirituality is NOT just religion. Some folks get in touch with their spirituality while hiking in the woods, flying down a long downhill on their bike or having meaningful discussions with friends and family. However, you connect with your spirituality, do it regularly and feel comfortable in your own skin.

Is Complacency Your Norm

While our understanding of disaster awareness and recovery expands, there is one indisputable fact regarding the response of most people to a tragedy or disaster. For the majority of people not directly touched by disaster, as time goes by the emotions of the event fade, and people tend to forget.

When your neighbor's house is burglarized, you immediately consider beefing up home security. But after a year, you have not installed a home security system, trimmed your shrubs to remove hiding places, kept porch lights on at night, or told your neighbors when you are planning a trip.

When Americans travel or visit public places, they constantly notice persons of suspect and wonder what are their intentions. But the thought passes quickly and they return to our lackadaisical enjoyment of our freedoms.

Crime scene at Aurora, Colorado theatre massacre 2012

Citizens hear of a mass shooting at a movie theater and for months avoid the movies thinking lightning will strike twice. Then when the latest blockbuster comes out, go in throngs. People see activities in their everyday lives that cause concern; kids bullying another child, accidents with seriously injured people, the hills on fire for miles, and are glad it is not affecting them. Having personally assisted police in closing off roads due to fatal auto accident investigations it is amazing the number of people who find such an event an annoyance. "How could someone die in a car accident here, that's how I go to the store and I'm going to be late!"

In my generation, almost everyone remembered where they were and what they were doing when President John F. Kennedy was assassinated in Dallas in 1963. Today, most have the same power of recollection for September 11, 2001 when terrorists forever changed New York City, a town in Pennsylvania, the Pentagon and our country. Since 9/11, our world has significantly changed, but what have you done to change your habits, routines and practices to accommodate the change?

Have you talked with your family about situational awareness and how to protect themselves in various locales? Do you wander about school, work, the mall, and entertainment venues completely oblivious to the individuals around you and potential dangers from them or the environment.

Are you part of the two-thirds of Americans that do not have an emergency plan for your family that addresses where to meet and how to communicate during or after an emergency event? If you are, you will probably panic like millions on 9/11 trying to make contact with family and loved ones, choking phone lines and calling 9-1-1 for help.

Have you expanded your sphere of friends and neighbors to increase your strength in numbers during an emergency? Or will you be on the 5 o'clock news crying with new found comrades in your neighborhood who lost everything in a fire, flood, tornado, or earthquake just like you.

Have you taken any concrete steps to improve your self-reliance should local emergency responders be unable to assist you? Or are you convinced that they, along with the Red Cross, will take care of you. If so, you need to re-read Chapter 2.

Have you learned any new skills to help you cope in the post 9/11 world? This may include such skills as self-defense, gardening, canning food, first aid or CPR. Did you know that FEMA has free interactive web-based courses including

- IS 10.a - Animals in Disasters: Awareness and Preparedness,
- IS 11.a - Animals in Disasters: Community Planning,
- IS 22 - Are You Ready?: An In-depth Guide to Citizen Preparedness,

- IS 244 - Developing and Managing Volunteers,
- IS 288- The Role of Volunteer Agencies in Emergency Management,
- IS 317 - Intro to Community Emergency Response Teams,
- IS 324 - Community Hurricane Preparedness, and
- IS 394.a - Protecting Your Home or Small Business in Disaster.

Have you improved your physical strength, endurance or body mass index? Being in "shape" is a significant indicator of one's ability to survive emergency situations. Could you walk 4-8 miles to a shelter? Can you carry your small child half way if they get tired? It is well proven that maintaining even a modicum level of fitness can improve your odds of survival in most situations.

Have you volunteered to help others? Many immediately after 9/11 jumped into volunteer services with a feeling of needing to do something. Take a fresh look at how you may be able to help others by volunteering your time. It could be with the Red Cross, your local Community Emergency Response Team (CERT), at a hospital, local police or sheriff, or even your church. Remember, many churches have very active disaster relief programs.

While memories of the last disaster fade, so does our resolution to get ready for the next big disaster. Empirical data clearly shows a significant rise in Google searches for earthquake kits the day after a major earthquake but two days later search traffic is back to normal and the concern/motivation is gone.

Disasters Hyped by the Media

Perhaps some of our complacency comes from the continuous cry of "Wolf" from the media. Americans hear about it every night on the national news. 56 million people in the path of some form of severe weather. Years' back you would have heard about a hurricane that hit the east coast or gulf region after the event. Now there is a week's warning of a possible hurricane. With advancing technology, the media can now predict how many Americans could be affected by the weather event. These weather events are so important to news ratings that such storms are immediately branded by the networks. "Superstorm Sandy," "Polar Vortex," "Arctic Blast," "Blizzard 2015," and "Flood Disaster" are a few examples. Are disasters being hyped by the media negatively affecting our personal disaster preparedness?

Certainly, the advanced warning is a tremendous accomplishment for meteorologists, useful for those directly affected, and great for TV news ratings. After all it was Paul Simon who sang "I get the news I need on the weather report" in the song *The Only Living Boy in New York*.

But while all this can be seen as good in terms of early warning, are people not becoming desensitized to the constant barrage of severe weather and the media hype? Is it really "national" news when a tornado hits a small town in Oklahoma decimating a dozen homes with no loss of life? Do we not expect some flooding near Fargo on the Red River (in recent years, the river has passed into flood stage at least once a year)? Are wildfires in California and Florida that unusual in the summer? Granted, due to the continued western drought, there is an early start to the fire season in California this year. But again, is a 2,000 acre wildfire in a small rural area of California where 50 homes are evacuated (and not lost) really "national" news?

The media loves a good fire. Not to diminish the impact on the lives of the people affected but, if there isn't an early morning fire in town the local NBC affiliate TV station will find one even if it is 2000 miles away in Savannah, GA, just to show us the smoke and flames!

While severe weather, especially in the east (where all the top news stations are headquartered) is often the lead story now days, would not the continued severe drought in the west be a bigger story? Boston did set a record for snowfall in the winter of 2014-15, but ultimately it melted and minimal local flooding resulted. While certainly inconvenient and difficult to get around town, it was just a temporary event.

The drought in California however is causing fewer crops to be planted which will reduce the overall food supply, less grass grown in pastures means less dairy cattle producing milk, and beef cattle producing summer hamburgers. With less supply for the same demand, prices will increase for everyone in the U.S., not just westerners! Now that's a lead national story for the media! However, 56 million people in the path of heavy rain takes the number one slot for several nights in a row.

So, while we may understand the need to *prepare for the unexpected*®, if we hear about severe weather every day, all of a sudden the definition of "severe" starts to become diluted to where citizens think "severe" means "normal." In fact, a local NBC affiliate station calls the daily weather report a "Weather Alert." Given that gripping title, what could they possibly call an impending severe weather event to get our attention?

Death by Ignorance

Ultimately disaster awareness is really all about reducing risk. Deep down inside everyone would like to think they are brazen gamblers that can win a fortune with the next lottery ticket. Millions have no problem plunking down $1 to $100 on lottery tickets when the pot gets huge (dwarfed only by the odds of winning). At times it seems people are like Wile E. Coyote always hoping for the best and a little taste of roadrunner dinner, but always coming up short.

Millions pour over their investment portfolios and retirement savings accounts to diversify them trying to minimize the risk of losing their life savings. The majority of Americans buy insurance for everything from earthquakes, floods, fire, to life, health and long-term care.

Yet, guarantee someone a 63% chance of not contracting the seasonal flu and possibly dying, and only 40% of Americans will insure that bet with a vaccination shot! Welcome to the modern day health concerns of the Center for Disease Control.

As Charles Darwin so eloquently stated, "It is not the strongest of the species that survives, nor the most intelligent that survives. It is the one that is most adaptable to change. In the struggle for survival, the fittest win out at the expense of their rivals because they succeed in adapting themselves best to their environment."

And it is also well documented that those who survive dangerous situations are the ones who are able to improvise and adapt to cover their basic needs. "Improvise, Adapt, Overcome" is also the unofficial slogan among U.S. Marines by no small accident. Whether you plan to bug in (shelter-in-place) or bug out (evacuate) given a disaster scenario, your ability to improvise, adapt, and overcome problems will be critical. Regardless of the size of your pantry, the amount of guns and ammo in your cache, the quality of your shelter, or your physical condition; you will still need more skills and creativity to survive.

Amanda Ripley concludes in her book, "all of us undergo a three-stage process when we find ourselves surviving a disaster: denial, deliberation and the 'decisive moment', during which the survivor buckles down and acts. The trick, may be to understand our instincts, which, in a crisis, may betray us. Some people run toward infernos, not away, and even in the face of obvious impending disaster, some people just won't move."[3]

As an example she cites, "Consider the World Trade Center (WTC) workers who, on Sept. 11, dithered at their desks, calling relatives, turning off computers and pondering which mementos to rescue from their desks even as the doomed jets burned above their heads." She went on to say, "those who made it out of the WTC waited an average of six minutes after the plane hit their building before heading for the exit and walking slowly — not running — down the stairs."[3]

"Quick-witted survivors are surprisingly anomalous. One fellow who made it through a horrific aircraft disaster in 1977 happened to be sitting on the runway reading an in-flight safety instruction card when another plane crashed into his. He grabbed his wife, leapt through a hole in the fuselage, and turned to see his fellow passengers remaining docilely in their seats, immobile. Most of them died within minutes as fire swept through the wreckage."[3]

Summary

Disaster awareness is so much more than just understanding the different types of disasters. It involves understanding the phases of any disaster and how you may react during each of those phases. With the understanding of what kind of behaviors can be expected, you should be able to take a more honest look at your own emotions and feel better knowing that you are not alone.

Disaster awareness is also about fighting complacency and not becoming desensitized to the constant barrage of severe weather and disasters heard about every day. Periodic training is a great way to continuously learn about disasters and prepare you for the mental and emotional challenges of a disaster.

References:

1. Counselling Connection, *Common Stages of Disaster Recovery*, Blog post, Professional Development, May 26, 2014, Retrieved from http://www.counsellingconnection.com/index.php/2014/05/26/common-stages-of-disaster-recovery/.
2. Carol S. North, MD, MPE, *Mental Health Response to Community Disasters: A Fact Sheet for Disaster Mental Health Planners, Responders, and Providers*, http://tdc.missouri.edu/doc/TDC_Community_MH_Response_FactSheet.pdf, Terrorism and

Disaster Center at the University of Missouri, 2014.

3. Amanda Ripley, *The Unthinkable: Who Survives When Disaster Strikes — And Why*, Potter/TenSpeed/Harmony, June 6, 2009.

4. Governing.com, The American Housing Survey, conducted by the Census Bureau and U.S. Department of Housing and Urban Development, 2013, http://www.governing.com/gov-data/safety-justice/emergency-preparedness-metro-areas-household-survey-data.html, Retrieved April 2, 2015.

Chapter 4 – Don't Focus on One Disaster

It never fails that when delivering an emergency preparedness and awareness presentation, someone always asks, "Why do we need emergency supplies? What can happen here?"

Well, consider the following events that have happened in small towns across America in 2014:

- Lincoln, CA – propane tanker fire evacuates thousands from their homes for a couple of days;
- Geiger, AL – tornado destroys 100 homes;
- Brattleboro, VT – epic flooding forced evacuations due to rainfall from the tail end of hurricane Irene;
- Bastrop, TX – wildfire, fanned by winds from tropical storm Lee, destroys nearly 500 homes; and
- Mineral, VA – 5.8 magnitude quake centered on this small east coast town.

By mid-April 2015 there were already 11 FEMA disaster declarations in the U.S., 45 in all of 2014, and 62 back in 2013! Texas, California, Oklahoma, New York and Florida lead the way in disaster declarations.

The ability of some folks to completely disregard the potential for a disaster to occur "anywhere" is amazing. These same people are seen on the 5 o'clock news saying "I never imagined something like this could happen here." It is really hard to feel sorry for folks who ignored all of the warnings and now want sympathy and support.

The purpose of this chapter is to expand your horizons and thoughts about disaster preparedness to include some local hazards you should consider during your emergency planning. Some of the more realistic hazards to consider will include:

- civil unrest,
- chemical attacks,
- earthquakes,
- electromagnetic pulse (EMP) attacks,
- floods,
- hazardous material incidents,
- heat waves,
- house fires,
- hurricanes,
- infectious diseases,
- nuclear explosions,
- power outages,
- terrorism,
- thunderstorms,
- tornadoes,
- tsunamis,
- water supply disruption,
- wildfires, and
- winter storms.

Realistic Hazards

Civil unrest – Civil disobedience exploded in the 60's and continues today with movements like

"Occupy Wall Street,", "Abortion Rights," and "Black Lives Matter." Citizens not directly involved in a civil unrest event may still have their lives significantly disrupted. Your ability to work, enjoy recreation, travel, and in some cases, obtain necessities may be jeopardized or delayed.

The disruption of infrastructure elements may also occur during very severe events. Public utilities such as water, fuel and electricity may be temporarily unavailable, as well as public infrastructure including roadways, phone lines and mobile communications. Once damaged, they cannot be repaired until the safety of repair workers can be assured. The inability of regularly scheduled food deliveries could significantly impact your dependence on your emergency supplies and pantry.

Occasionally, the disruption of such services may be the original cause of the unrest. More frequently, the cause of such issues is related to economic stagnation, severe inflation, devaluation of currency, disasters man-made or natural, severe unemployment, oppression, political scandal, or, sporting events. For short duration unrest, sheltering-in-place is usually best; however, longer-term or more violent unrest may precipitate evacuations.

Chemical attacks – This is a terrifying but plausible scenario. You're in an enclosed crowded place—perhaps a subway or a mall—and a terrorist organization releases lethal quantities of a nerve agent such as sarin into the air. The gas sends your nervous system into overdrive. You begin having convulsions.

EMTs rush to the scene while you go into respiratory failure.

Chemical attacks by terrorists are not hypothetical. The Aum Shinrikyo group in Japan used sarin gas to attack subway passengers twice: an attack in 1994 killed eight people and a second attack in 1995 killed 12. Experts agree that these attacks were amateurish and a better timed and executed attack could have killed many more people.

The CDC has a Strategic National Stockpile "CHEMPACK" program where they store chemical attack antidotes. 1,960 CHEMPACKs are strategically placed in more than 1,340 locations in all states, territories, island jurisdictions, and the District of Columbia. Most are located in hospitals or fire stations selected by local authorities to support a rapid hazmat response. More than 90% of the U.S. population is within one hour of a CHEMPACK location, and if hospitals or first responders need them, they can be accessed quickly.

Larger cities would be preferred targets because simply put, there are not a lot of headlines to be made by launching a chemical attack in Pickstown, SD with its population of 210. If you are lucky enough to live near a CHEMPAK location when you are exposed, first responders should have an antidote for you. Those not directly in the attack area (hot zone) should shelter-in-place and prevent the toxin from entering their safe room. If you do not live within one hour of such a location, you hopefully would not experience an attack.

Earthquakes – Mother Nature does her part to remind all of us about the hazards that earthquakes bring. The following events occurred on August 1, 2014:

- Tacoma, WA – 3.5 magnitude earthquake;
- Cherokee, OK – 3.4 magnitude earthquake;
- Gabbs, NV – 3.1 magnitude earthquake;
- Lakeview, OR – 3.0 magnitude earthquake;
- Loma Linda, CA – 2.1 magnitude earthquake;
- Athens, TN – 2.0-magnitude earthquake; and
- California recorded 731 earthquakes in the week preceding August 1!

We now know that earthquakes are occurring more frequently in parts of the U.S. where they have historically been rare (see Figure 1). This means that many people around the country who have no earthquake preparedness plans are now vulnerable.

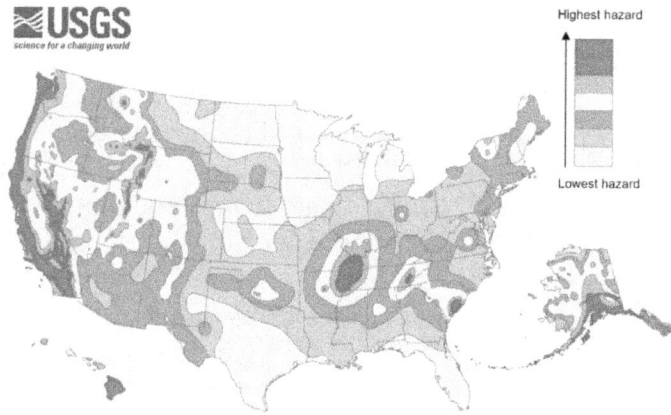

Figure 1 – 2014 USGS National Seismic Hazard Map

A recent U.S. Geological Survey's (USGS) update to the U.S. National Seismic Hazard Maps (shown above), shows that earthquake hazard in the central U.S. and on the east coast is higher than previously thought. Among the highest-risk states: Missouri and Tennessee which were the site of the 1811-12 New Madrid quakes that rerouted the Mississippi River.

With input from more than 150 scientists, the USGS released a separate earthquake hazard map for "man-made" earthquakes. The map (see Figure 2) highlights 17 hotspots where communities face a significantly increased risk of earthquakes, and the accompanying report linked the earthquakes to wastewater injection wells. Previous maps did not include earthquakes that are induced by human activities.[1]

The updated map shows that fracking's byproducts are clearly to blame for swarms of earthquakes plaguing several states. The earthquake hotspots include the states of Oklahoma, Kansas, Texas, Ohio, Arkansas, Alabama, Colorado and New Mexico.[1]

Hydraulic fracturing, or "fracking", extracts far more water from these underground oil-laden rocks than traditional drilling. Currently, there is no way to treat, store and release the billions of gallons of wastewater at the surface. Instead, drillers pump the fluid back underground, below groundwater, where it sometimes triggers earthquakes. Oklahoma's current earthquake rate is now 600 times higher than its pre-fracking rate, which was based on the state's natural seismicity.[1]

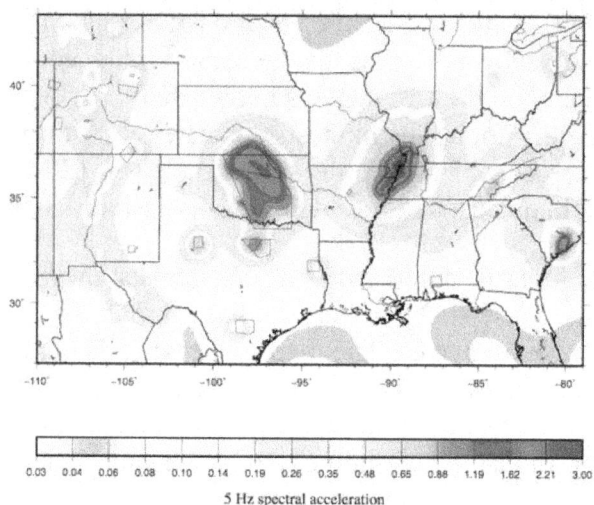

B) 0.04%/yr test case with a declustered catalog and 50 km smoothing; combined with the 2014 NSHM

0.03 0.04 0.06 0.08 0.10 0.14 0.19 0.26 0.35 0.48 0.65 0.86 1.19 1.82 2.21 3.00

5 Hz spectral acceleration

Figure 2 – "Man-made Earthquakes 2015

However, in terms of earthquakes, some places may be safer to live than others in the United States. From 1975 to 1995 there were only four states that did not have any earthquakes - Florida, Iowa, North Dakota, and Wisconsin.

During an earthquake, the best course of action depends upon your location.

- **Inside** – Stay inside in a structurally protected location, avoiding areas with heavy overhead objects (e.g. home heating units, overhead lighting fixtures, etc.), and protecting your head. If the structure you are in exhibits heavy damage and appears unstable leave the structure ONLY after the shaking has stopped. Care should be taken to avoid falling objects from outside or above the structure (e.g. brick chimneys, air conditioning units, roof tiles, etc.)

- **Outside** – Stay outside and ensure your location is not near any buildings or tall structures (e.g. telephone poles, power lines, bill boards, etc.) that could fall on you.
- **In your car** – Stay in your car. If driving, slow down and pull over as safely as possible and consider your surroundings as noted in "Outside" above. Your car will provide some protection from falling objects so remain in it until you are able to continue on safely. Pay close attention to road hazard warnings via the radio.

EMP attacks – This is not a bogus event! An Electromagnetic Pulse (EMP) Attack is a real phenomenon and concern in today's electronic world. Back in April 2008, a report by the Commission to Assess the Threat to the United States from Electromagnetic Pulse (EMP) Attack – Critical National Infrastructures stated in regards to such an attack, "The consequences of lack of food, heat (or air conditioning), water, waste disposal, medical, police, fire fighting support, and effective civil authority would threaten society itself."

What could cause and EMP Attack? The most probable causes would be naturally occurring solar flares and coronal mass ejections or a man-made high altitude nuclear explosion. As a result of an EMP attack, electromagnetic radiation and energetic particles can temporarily alter the upper atmosphere creating disruptions with radio signal transmission. Such disruptions can cause computer operated devices (from cell phones and laptops to automobiles and airplanes) as well as Supervisory Control and Data Acquisition (SCADA) systems to fail. Such SCADA systems run most large manufacturing, processing and transportation systems in the U.S. Imagine if water treatment plants were unable to treat drinking water, oil refineries lost the ability to process crude oil into gasoline, the power grid failed and blackouts spread on a regional scale, and transportation monitoring systems failed causing accidents that blocked major roads and highways impacting the delivery of everything you buy on a weekly basis. Generally, an EMP attack is a shelter-in-place event.

Floods – Of all the natural disasters Mother Nature flings at us, a flood is the most common and the most devastating – personally, financially and often physically. In the United States alone, floods hold the distinction of being the country's "deadliest" weather condition, with about 200 deaths attributed to the disaster every year.

Floods are deadliest weather events in U.S.

Very few areas are completely free from the threat of a flood, even in the most arid regions of the country. The Federal Emergency Management Agency (FEMA) has placed more than 20,000 communities in the United States into a category of flood zones. The most hazardous flood zones are classified as "V" (usually first-row, beach-front properties) and "A" (usually, but not always, properties near water).

Flooding can be caused by a variety of processes including overland or overbank flooding, flash floods, coastal flooding, ice jam flooding and structural failures (such as levees and dams which will be discussed further in the Water Supply Disruption section). Floods can be limited to a particular community or they can be widespread, affecting entire cities and valleys or large portions of states. While they can develop quickly; the majority of the time local meteorologists are able to alert you to heavy rain or snow melt ahead of the actual event. Many residents insist on staying either in an attempt to protect their property or they do not believe the flood will be severe. However, once pre-flood activities have been completed around your home, most would do well to evacuate ahead of the water.

Hazardous material (HAZMAT) incidents – No one ever considers that a HAZMAT spill could happen near them unless they live near a chemical plant or refinery. But those same commodities are transported all over the U.S. via rail and road every day through towns large and small. In particular, exploding oil trains are a hot topic in the U.S. spurred by a recent spate of accidents and a prediction by the U.S. Department of Transportation last year that there are many more to come – 10 a year over the next two decades.

Trains derailing, trains hitting tanker trucks, tanker trucks involved in multi-car pile ups on freeways, and other freak accidents happen every day. Most people are completely unaware of the extent of HAZMAT traffic in their towns. While these events typically require a shelter-in-place response to protect against hazardous smoke or gas, many have occurred near waterways and contaminated local drinking water for weeks. This is exactly what happened in Kanawha County, WV in January of 2014 when a toxic liquid (4-methylcyclohexane methanol) leaked from a storage tank at a Freedom Industries facility. Other incidents may require evacuations due to the toxic smoke caused when HAZMAT products must burn themselves out.

Heat waves – Heat can affect anyone. However, it is more likely to adversely affect young children, the elderly, and people with health problems. People who have medical conditions that cause poor blood circulation, those who take diuretics (water pills that help the body get rid of unneeded water and salt through the urine), and those with certain skin conditions may be more susceptible to heat.

However, heat waves and the increased demand on the electrical grid can also cause rolling brownouts or blackouts. Therefore you need to be prepared for potential power outages and how to stay cool. Extensive heat waves or droughts like the one currently gripping the West for the fourth straight year can have devastating effects on crop production.

Remember to consider your pets and animals too. Ensure they have a cool place out of the direct sunlight to rest. Do not encourage excessive play or work activities for an animal on hot days and make sure they have access to plenty of fresh cool water to keep them hydrated. Generally heat waves with high local heat indexes require most people to shelter-in-place and stay cool.

House fire results in total loss

House fires – In 2013, there were 487,500 structure fires, causing 2,855 civilian deaths, 14,075 civilian injuries, and $9.5 billion in property damage. One home structure fire was reported every 85 seconds. Table 1 below identifies the latest data for type and quantity of home fire incidents between 2007 and 2011.[2]

Table 1

Type of Fire Incident	Total Incidents
Cooking	156,600
Grill including outside fires	8,800
Heating	60,420
Structure smoking-material	17,600

Electrical distribution and lighting (not electrical failures)	22,600
Child play	7,100
Outside child play	37,400
Lightning	22,600
Candle fires	10,630
Christmas tree fires	230
Intentional fires	28,900

Make sure you and your family have an emergency exit plan for a house fire including at least 2 ways out of every room. It is also crucial to have a family meeting place in case of a house fire where you can all meet in the event you are separated during your escape.

Hurricanes – All Atlantic and Gulf of Mexico coastal areas are subject to hurricanes. Parts of the Southwest U.S. and the Pacific Coast experience heavy rains and floods each year from hurricanes. The Atlantic hurricane season occurs from June to November with the peak season from mid-August to late October.

Hurricanes can cause severe damage to coastlines and structures hundreds of miles inland and are classified into five categories (1-5) based on wind speed, pressure, and damage potential. Category 3, 4 and 5 hurricanes are considered major. Category 1 and 2 are dangerous and require your attention.

The most common advice to survive a hurricane is to take the days of warning from meteorologists to heart and evacuate to a safer location ahead of the storm. Sheltering-in-place is not considered a good strategy for a hurricane.

Infectious diseases – Many infectious diseases have been identified and monitored over the years. Some are more virulent than others but all can become extremely deadly if not properly managed, contained, and treated. Approximately half of all deaths caused by infectious diseases each year can be attributed to just three diseases: tuberculosis, malaria, and AIDS. Together, these diseases cause over 300 million illnesses and more than 5 million deaths each year. Many of the infectious diseases are more prevalent in other countries, but here in the U.S. the more common ones we live with every day include

- **Cryptosporidiosis**: - is caused by a parasite that spreads when a water source is contaminated, usually with the feces of infected animals or humans.
- **Hepatitis**: - is a group of liver diseases known by type A, B and C. Approximately 2 billion people are infected with the hepatitis B virus (HBV), making it the most common infectious disease in the world today.

- **HIV/AIDS**: - the human immunodeficiency virus (HIV) that causes Acquired Immune Deficiency Syndrome (AIDS).
- **Influenza**: - most often talked about when discussing a pandemic.
- **Measles**: - is a disease that has seen a drastic reduction in countries where a vaccine is readily available; however, recent increased cases in the U.S. are being attributed to children who were not vaccinated.
- **Meningitis**: - often known as spinal meningitis, is an infection of the spinal cord. It is usually the result of a viral or bacterial infection. Over 10% of all cases are fatal.
- **Pneumonia**: - is usually an infection of the streptococcus or mycoplasma bacteria. These bacteria can live in the human body without causing infection for years, and only surface when another illness has lowered the person's immunity to disease.
- **Strep Throat**: - is caused by the streptococcus bacteria. Several million cases of strep throat occur every year.
- **Tuberculosis**: - cause nearly 2 million deaths every year.

The globalization of society, air travel, and terrorism all provide the potential to spread diseases that are more prevalent in other countries to the U.S. Instead of a suicide bomber consider how a suicide disease host could rapidly expose hundreds and severely impact our lives. Some of these diseases include

- **Ebola**: - previously known as Ebola hemorrhagic fever, is a rare and deadly disease caused by infection with one of the Ebola virus strains. Learn how to reduce your risk at the Ebola Response Resource Site.
- **Marburg**: - a virus similar to Ebola, which has recently hit the radar in the African country of Uganda, raising concerns about another deadly outbreak there.
- **SARS**: - Severe acute respiratory syndrome (SARS) is a viral respiratory illness caused by a coronavirus. SARS was first reported in Asia in February 2003. Since 2004, there have not been any known cases of SARS reported anywhere in the world. Despite this, on October 5, 2012, the National Select Agent Registry Program published a final rule declaring SARS a select agent that has the potential to pose a severe threat to public health and safety.

However, experts currently believe the three most threatening infections to the U.S. are:

- **Influenza**: - see Pandemic Preparedness and Flu Safety.
- **MRSA**: - methicillin-resistant Staphylococcus aureus, or MRSA, is a strain of staph bacteria that does not respond to the antibiotics traditionally used to treat the infection.
- **Resistant Gonorrhea**: - an estimated 246,000 cases of resistant gonorrhea crop up in the U.S. each year.

Nuclear explosions – Back in the Cold War days, everyone knew how to duck and cover during a nuclear explosion. But since then little attention has been paid to such an attack and how to survive a nuclear explosion. Suppose the unthinkable happened, and terrorists struck New York or another big city with a nuclear bomb. What should people there do? The government has a surprising new message: Do not flee. Get inside any stable building and do not come out until officials say it is safe.[3]

Mushroom cloud following nuclear test in the South Pacific

Now after decades of government concern and our lack of concern, the new message is citizen preparedness. For people who survive the initial blast, the main advice is to fight the impulse to run and instead seek shelter from the lethal radioactivity. Even a few hours of protection, officials say, can greatly increase survival rates. "We have to get past the mental block that says it's too terrible to think about," W. Craig Fugate, administrator of the Federal Emergency Management Agency, said in an interview. "We have to be ready to deal with it" and help people learn how to "best protect themselves." [3]

The advice is based on recent scientific analyses showing that a nuclear attack is much more survivable if you immediately shield yourself from the lethal radiation that follows a blast, a simple tactic seen as saving hundreds of thousands of lives. Even staying in a car, the studies show, would reduce casualties by more than 50 percent; hunkering down in a basement would be better by far. [3]

Administration officials argue that the cold war created an unrealistic sense of fatalism about a terrorist nuclear attack. "It's more survivable than most people think," said an official deeply involved in the planning, who spoke on the condition of anonymity. "The key is avoiding nuclear fallout." [3]

Peter Bergen, a fellow at the New America Foundation and New York University's Center on Law and Security, recently argued that the odds of any terrorist group obtaining a nuclear weapon are "near zero for the foreseeable future." But another school says that the potential consequences are so high that the administration is, if anything, being too timid. [3]

The Department of Homeland Security financed a multi-agency modeling effort led by the Lawrence Livermore National Laboratory in California. The scientists looked at Washington, New York, Chicago,

Los Angeles and other big cities, using computers to simulate details of the urban landscape and terrorist bombs. The results were revealing. For instance, the scientists found that a bomb's flash would blind many drivers, causing accidents and complicating evacuation routes. The big surprise was how taking shelter for as little as several hours made a huge difference in survival rates. [3]

Power outages – The primary cause of power outages in the U.S. is severe weather and that has cost the economy $18 billion to $33 billion a year on average from 2003 to 2012 when adjusted for inflation, according to a report from the White House and Energy Department.

Additionally, the report stated, "The number of outages caused by severe weather is expected to rise as climate change increases the frequency and intensity of hurricanes, blizzards, floods and other extreme weather events."

However, there are other issues looming that could increase the number of power outages around the country.

- **Aging Grid** - The U.S. electrical grid is an interconnected network for delivering electricity from suppliers (generally utility companies) to consumers. It consists of 5800 power plants that produce electrical power; 450,000 miles of high-voltage transmission lines that carry power from distant sources (power plants) to demand centers (your city);

and distribution lines that connect to individual customers (your house). Utility executives identified aging infrastructure as the number one challenge facing the electric industry according to a recent Utility Dive survey. This challenge easily tops an aging workforce, regulatory models, and stagnant load growth.[4]

- **Low Cost Natural Gas** - Our growing reliance on natural gas-fired generation could also create weak spots in the grid. For example, utilities that supply natural gas to customers for heat can usually take all the gas they need from pipelines before any excess goes to electricity generators. In regions with limited pipeline capacity, such as the Northeast, planners say there might not be enough gas to simultaneously heat homes and generate electricity during a cold snap.

- **Power Plant Shutdowns** - The bulk power system is changing; a result of the declining use of coal and nuclear power and the rising use of natural gas and renewable power. One-sixth of the existing coal capacity is projected to be taken off-line by 2020, much of it at small, inefficient units in the Ohio River Valley, the Mid-Atlantic and the Southeast, according to the Energy Information Administration. The permanent closure of four nuclear reactors in California, Florida and Wisconsin was announced this year, and reactors in New York, Vermont and elsewhere may also close. Plant shutdowns mean there is less of a cushion in electrical capacity when power demand is high or problems arise. These shutdowns can also create pockets of transmission congestion or regions where power is scarce. Both situations drive up power prices for customers, make the grid less stable, and present planning challenges.

- **Cyber Threats** - The US electrical grid is under constant attack from malware and cyber-criminals, yet most utility companies implement only the bare minimum of security standards, according to a new report released by Congressmen Ed Markey (D-MA) and Henry Waxman (D-CA). Markey said, "National security experts say that cyber-attacks on America's electric grid top the target list for terrorists and rogue states (e.g., China, North Korea, Russia), yet we remain highly vulnerable to attacks." Among the report's findings, "more than a dozen utilities surveyed said their systems were under "daily," "frequent," or "constant" attack, with one claiming to be the target of around 10,000 attempted cyber-attacks each month."

It does not take a tremendously powerful storm to cause a widespread power outage, but storms are only a portion of the ways our electrical grid can be compromised. Regardless of the cause, you should be making plans now to withstand a power outage before the next one occurs.

Terrorism – The potential for terrorism is not new and is defined as the use of force or violence against persons or property in violation of the criminal laws of a nation. The purpose of terrorism is to intimidate, coerce, or cause ransom. Terrorist acts are designed to create fear in the public, show a government is powerless, and get publicity for the terrorist's causes.

World Trade Center Collapse, New York, NY, September 11, 2001

As we have become aware, acts of terrorism include threats of terrorism; assassinations; kidnappings; hijackings; bomb scares and bombings; and cyber-attacks. Terrorist weapons of mass destruction include Chemical weapons; Biological agents, Radiological dispersion devices, Nuclear weapons and Explosive devices (referred to as CBRNE). However when rated from the least risk to the greatest risk, the weapons are ranked like this:

- nuclear,

- chemical,
- radiological,
- biological, and
- explosives.

The weapon of choice for terrorists, which is said to have been used in 80% of such attacks are explosives, specifically high-yield explosives. This includes military munitions: grenades, mortars, surface-to-air missiles, and improvised explosive devices or IEDs.

The goal of terrorists is to cause mass casualties, affect critical resources, disrupt vital services, disrupt economies, and heighten fear. Key targets include seats of government, key industries, bridges, subways, tunnels, and other key transportation facilities.

While your constant vigilance and attention to everyday activities around you can be a significant deterrent to terrorist acts when reported, there is little else you can control. The key to including terrorist activities in your emergency plan is to consider how you and your family should react in a given situation relative to sheltering-in-place or evacuating, and how and where you can communicate or meet up after such an event.

Thunderstorms – On average, lightning kills 60 to 80 Americans each year making it the second most dangerous severe weather event while flooding is number one. Eighty percent of all lightning deaths are male. However, only ten percent of persons struck by lightning die, with cardiac arrest essentially being the only immediate cause, other than from a secondary cause such as a fall or collision with a rock after being struck first. Of the hundred others who are struck by lightning annually and survive, many incur debilitating lifelong injuries, especially to their neurological functions.

Severe thunderstorm and lightning

Based on reported data, the odds that people living in America will be struck by lightning are about one in 700,000. Those that live where there are numerous thunderstorms and who spend a lot of time outdoors are at much higher risk. From 1990 through 2003, the most lightning deaths each year occurred in Florida - twice as many as in any other state - followed by Texas, Colorado, Ohio and North Carolina.

When lightning will strike is completely unpredictable. It can unleash a bolt ten miles ahead of a storm. Because people typically do not take precautions before a storm or in the period shortly after it leaves, these times are the most dangerous. Lightning can strike even when the skies are blue. Because every bolt originates in a storm cloud, one can exit from a concealed cloud (e.g., a cloud behind a mountain ridge) and literally streak sideways to hit something miles away. There is no safe interval between one bolt and the next; the second may follow almost immediately. The distance between one lightning strike and the next in a sequence of strikes can be six to eight miles. When you can hear thunder, even distant thunder, the next lightning bolt could still strike you.

The outdoors is the most dangerous place to be during a lightning storm. At the first indication of an impending storm, go inside to a completely enclosed building (not a carport, open garage or covered patio) or into a hard-top vehicle. If you are caught outdoors and cannot get to an enclosed building, seek the lowest point and be the lowest point in the surrounding terrain. You do not want to be the tallest or second tallest object during a lightning storm. If in an open area, crouch down on the balls of your feet making as little contact with the ground as possible.

You should also avoid

- tall trees (be at least twice as far from a tall tree as the height of the tree);

- small caves (a large cave can offer safety but only if one stays in the middle away from the walls);
- rock enclosures, outcroppings and "chimney" rocks - each can become a death trap if lightning strikes in the vicinity;
- being near or touching any metal;
- large groups (stay several yards away from other people), and
- standing in puddles, or being in small boats or canoes.

Tornadoes – Unlike hurricanes, tornadoes do not have a "season" per se. However, March to December can be considered a high probability time frame for tornadoes.

Most of the early spring tornadoes in the U.S. tend to occur in the Southeast and South Central regions also referred to as "Dixie Alley." Gulf States, such as Mississippi and Louisiana are the frequent recipients of tornadoes from February to April. Late spring tornadoes generally spread a bit farther north, often into Kansas, Nebraska and the Tennessee Valley region generally referred to as "Tornado Alley." By mid-summer, most of Tornado Alley is active and tornadoes may occur throughout the U.S. Late summer tends to bring some of the stronger tornadoes into the upper Midwest and Ohio valleys, and the pattern shifts back southward into the late autumn to Dixie Alley.

The actual average number of tornadoes is unknown, recent trends indicate the number is close to 1,300. In

2011 there were 1,894 tornadoes recorded in the U.S resulting in 550 deaths and $28.7 billion in damages. On average, about 60 people are killed by tornadoes every year, most from flying or falling debris.

Remember to do the following before a tornado hits:

- Determine the best location in your home and place of employment in which to seek shelter when threatened by a tornado. A basement or cellar will usually afford the best protection. If an underground shelter is not available, identify an interior room or hallway on the lowest floor to ride out the winds.
- Conduct periodic tornado safety drills with your family.
- If you live in tornado prone areas, you should know the locations of designated shelters in places where you and your family spend time, such as public buildings, nursing homes and shopping centers.
- Learn how to shut off the power, gas and water to your home.
- Make an inventory of your possessions. Take photographs or videotape your belongings. Keep records in a safe deposit box or some other location away from the residence.

Tsunamis – These are a series of enormous waves created by an underwater disturbance such as an earthquake, landslide, volcanic eruption, or meteorite impact. The word, pronounced "soo-ná-mees" comes from the Japanese word where " tsu" means "harbor" and "nami" means "wave." Tsunamis are also referred to as seismic sea waves (mistakenly called "tidal waves").

These waves travel outward in all directions from the area of disturbance as fast as 500 miles per hour, similar to the ripples you see when you throw a pebble in open water. As the waves approach shallow waters along the coast they grow in height (up to 100 feet) depending on the topography of the coastline and the ocean floor. A good indication of a large wave approaching is when the ocean recedes from the beach. If you see this, get to higher ground immediately.

Tsunamis can strike anywhere along most of the U.S. coastline but Hawaii has the greatest risk. This state has about one a year, with a damaging tsunami happening about every seven years. Alaska is also at high risk. Coastal states, like California, Oregon and Washington experience a damaging tsunami about every 18 years. Areas are at greater risk if they are less than 25 feet above sea level and within a mile of the shoreline. According to FEMA, drowning is the most common cause of death associated with a tsunami.

To ensure the early detection of tsunamis, the National Oceanic Atmospheric Administration (NOAA) has placed Deep-ocean Assessment and Reporting of Tsunami (DART®) stations in regions with a history of generating destructive tsunamis including the Aleutian Islands and the west coast of the U.S. While these warning systems are in place world-wide, available civilian reaction time depends solely on the proximity of the underwater disturbance to the coastline. Off the coast of Hokkaidō, Japan a tsunami struck the small island of Okushiri, Hokkaido within three to five minutes after a magnitude 7.7 earthquake shook the sea bed on July 12, 1993. A similar "near coastline" earthquake caused the devastating Aceh, Indonesia tsunami on December 26, 2004. On the other hand, the resulting tsunami wave from the 2011 Tohoku earthquake in Japan took approximately 30 hours to impact the Oregon coast.

Prior to a tsunami you should

- know the height of your street above sea level and the distance of your street from the coast as evacuation orders may be based on these numbers,
- make sure your go bags are stocked with fresh supplies and ready for evacuation,
- talk to family members about your tsunami evacuation and communication plans,
- understand school evacuation plans and how you will pick up your children from school or from another location,
- know your community's warning systems and potential evacuation routes, and
- turn on your radio to the Emergency Alert System following an earthquake to hear if a tsunami warning has been issued.

Following a tsunami warning

- follow the evacuation orders issued by authorities and evacuate immediately with your pets,
- move inland to higher ground (at least 2 miles and 100 feet above sea level if possible), and
- stay away from the beach.

Water supply disruption - Without question, readily available water and electricity are the two utilities most people are not prepared to do without. An emergency water supply is the most critical element of a disaster plan that most folks just forget about. Each person needs one gallon per day of stored water for an emergency, but what about having more than three days' worth of water supply? Look around at how fragile our water supplies really are. Flooding, aging water systems and terrorism provide the most incentive to plan your emergency water supply now. Consider the following

- Local vandals opened two fire hydrants and drained Hamlet, Indiana's water tower of over 300,000 gallons of water resulting in a "boil water" order.
- Local flooding due to a water main break in Miami-Dade County, Florida resulted in a "boil water" order and the power being shut off to a neighborhood for two days.
- May 2010, a major pipe bringing water to the Boston area sprung a "catastrophic" leak and forced over two million people to boil water for three days.
- The Association of State Dam Safety Officials has found that the number of dams in the

United States that could fail has grown 134% since 1999 to 3,346.

- More than a third of all dam failures or near failures since 1874 happened in just the last decade.
- The amount of rain falling in the heaviest downpours has increased approximately 20 percent on average in the past century.[5] This does not include the deluges in May 2015 throughout Texas and Oklahoma which caused widespread flooding.

Generally speaking, floods are the result of levee failures, dam failures, excessive rain fall, or snow melt. When flooding occurs it can easily inundate local water treatment plants leaving them unable to keep untreated water out of the system or it forces the shutdown of the plant. Here is a closer look at each of the main causes of flooding.

1. Levees – The number of levees in the United States it is estimated at more than 30,000 miles. They exist in every state and the Federal Emergency Management Agency (FEMA) estimates that levees are found in approximately 22% of the nation's 3,147 counties. Forty-three percent of the U.S. population lives in counties with levees.

   Many of these levees were designed decades ago to protect agricultural and rural areas, not the homes and businesses that are now located behind them. While some are multimillion-dollar concrete systems many are nothing more than piles of sand and dirt created by farmers as barricades against rising rivers that cyclically destroyed their crops.

In February 2007, the U.S. Army Corps of Engineers released the locations of levees determined to have unacceptable maintenance inspection ratings. Levees in more than 80 cities and townships in 27 states were identified as having one or more deficient conditions, including animal burrows, erosion, tree growth, floodwall movement or faulty culverts, any of which could prevent the structure from functioning as designed.[6]

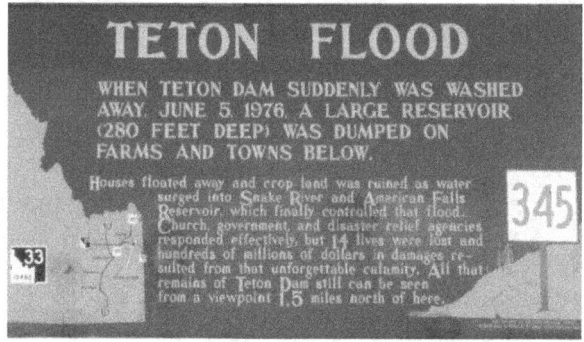

Teton earthen dam failure marker in Idaho

2. Dams – The National Inventory of Dams, which is maintained by the U.S. Army Corps of Engineers shows that the number

of dams that are more than 25 feet high, hold more than 50 acre-feet of water, or are considered a significant hazard if they fail was at 87,000. However, the federal government owns or regulates only 6% of those dams.[7] Responsibility for ensuring the safety of 77% (66,990) of the nation's dams falls to state dam safety programs. Many state dam safety programs do not have sufficient resources, funding, or staff to conduct dam safety inspections. For example, Iowa has only three engineers and an annual budget of $140,000 to regulate more than 3,927 dams. Each inspector is responsible for more than 1,287 dams! Worse still, Alabama does not have a dam safety program despite the fact that there are more than 2,000 dams in the state. In some states many dams are specifically exempted from inspection by state law.[8]

Many dams are determined to be deficient as a result of aging, deterioration, and a lack of maintenance. Dams are now being deemed unsafe or deficient as a result of increased scientific and engineering knowledge about large flood events and earthquake re-mapping; and the ability to predict a dam's structural response to such extreme events, which pose a significant safety threat.

The average age of our nation's dams is 52 years. By 2020, 70% of the total dams in the

United States will be over 50 years old. Fifty years ago dams were built with the best engineering and construction standards of the time. However, as the scientific and engineering data have improved, many dams are not expected to safely withstand current predictions regarding large floods and earthquakes. In addition, many of these dams were initially constructed using less-stringent design criteria for low-hazard dams due to the lack of development below the dam.[9]

While the total number of dams is increasing, the number of high hazard potential dams is also increasing at an alarming rate, now totaling 13,991 as of 2012. The term "high-hazard" does not necessarily mean the dam is deficient, but instead that the consequences are expected to include loss of life should the dam fail. That represents an increase of more than 3,873 new high hazard potential dams since 2002. This increase is a result of new residential and commercial developments below dams, which is dramatically increasing the consequences of failure and resulting in the reclassification of dams. This change in classification requires that significantly greater safety standards be met given the greater consequences of dam failure.[9].

3.   Rainfall/Snowmelt – In just 2010, FEMA issued 90 Emergency and Major Disaster Declarations in the United States. Of these, 60% (or 54 declarations) involved flooding due to severe storms or unseasonably warm weather. Ten years earlier in 2000, there were 50 combined Emergency and Major Disaster Declarations in the United States. Of those, 38% (or 19 declarations) involved flooding.

Flooding often occurs when heavy precipitation persists for weeks to months in large river basins. Such extended periods of heavy precipitation have been increasing over the past century, most notably in the past two to three decades in the United States. For the future, precipitation intensity is projected to increase everywhere, with the largest increases occurring in areas in which average precipitation increases the most. For example, the Midwest and Northeast, where total precipitation is expected to increase the most, would also experience the largest increases in heavy precipitation events.[5]

Weather Channel meteorologist Tom Moore cites urbanization and land-use changes as a cause for what appears to be the increased flooding across the USA. "In the metro areas, flooding just gets worse each decade," he says. "Because we're stripping trees and grasses away, the runoff is quicker and more extreme. These areas are now far more vulnerable to flooding."[10]

The public's awareness of our nation's aging water infrastructure was measured by ITT Corporation's Value of Water Survey, a nationwide poll taken in late 2010. Not surprisingly, the survey showed that many are concerned about our water system. But Colin Sabol, vice president of marketing and business development in ITT's Fluid and Motion Control division, says "since we can't see the underground pipes, they don't get as much attention as, say, potholes."

According to the report, every day there are 650 water main breaks in the U.S. As reported by the American Society of Civil Engineers, leaking pipes lose an estimated seven billion gallons of clean drinking water a day. This is the amount of water that the top 10 cities consume in a year. If you could take all the leaks and feed it into one faucet it would take care of our top 10 cities. Those areas that were developed over 100 years ago—the Northeast and Midwest—tend to have older infrastructure. The EPA estimates that over 240,000 water main breaks occur per year in the U.S. in some 1.8 million miles of water distribution lines.

Even back in 1941, Federal Bureau of Investigation Director J. Edgar Hoover wrote, "It has long been recognized that among public utilities, water supply facilities offer a particularly vulnerable point of attack to the foreign agent, due to the strategic position they occupy in keeping the wheels of industry turning and in preserving the health and morale of the American populace." Water infrastructure systems also are highly linked with other infrastructures, especially electric power and transportation, as well as the chemical industry which supplies treatment chemicals, making security of all of them an issue of concern.

The Congressional Research Service reported back in 2003 that "The September 11, 2001, attacks on the World Trade Center and the Pentagon have drawn attention to the security of many institutions, facilities, and systems in the United States, including the nation's water supply and water quality infrastructure. These systems have long been recognized as being potentially vulnerable to terrorist attacks of various types, including bioterrorism/chemical contamination, physical disruption, and cyber-attack."

- **Biological/Chemical Contamination** – Many feel that a terrorist attack which places chemicals or even biological agents in the water supply is unlikely to be successful. Contamination of a reservoir with a biological agent would not likely produce a large risk to public health because of the dilution effect. These reservoirs contain hundreds of thousands or even millions of gallons of water. A massive amount of contaminant would be required for a successful terrorist attack at this point. If agents were to be introduced at this point they are likely to be detected and unlikely to survive the chlorination process. Even so, filtration and disinfection of the water may occur downstream mitigating the contamination. However, if the point of contamination is after a treatment facility where filters, chlorination, and other preventative measures would no longer be effective; the likelihood of success is much greater. Fortunately, this type of act is still subject to the dilution issue which would lessen the severity of such an attack.

- **Physical Disruption** – A more effective means of affecting our water supply would be damaging physical water system components (e.g., piping, pumps, holding tanks, etc.). This could restrict the available drinking water supply from reaching households in the water system area. Local businesses would not be able to conduct operations, manufacturing could be stalled, food service stores would close, and everyday life depending on fresh water would be in disarray. In some communities the drinking water is also used to supply fire hydrants. Without this water supply, a fire department's ability to fight fires would be impossible.

- **Cyber Attacks** – Cyber-attacks are another potential threat to disrupt our water service. Computer networks and digital monitoring technology (SCADA systems) play a key role in the management of our nation's water supplies. United States law enforcement and intelligence agencies have previously received credible indications that al-Qaida members have sought information on SCADA systems available on multiple SCADA-related web sites.

Wildfires – Droughts, prolonged heat, and dry conditions increase the risk for wildfires and California just declared that fire season is now year-round. The careless use of fire in highly wooded residential, industrial, or camping areas can also dramatically increase the chance of a wildfire. Flames can quickly spread across trees and dry brush, threatening homes and businesses, both in the immediate vicinity and further along the path of the fire.

Helping your home and property survive a wildfire entails about 99 percent preparation. Once a wildfire is born, it moves fast and can change direction literally on the shift of a breeze. Here are several important steps to take on and around your property that may prevent or lessen the damage from a wildfire:

- Design and landscape your home with wildfire safety in mind. Select materials and plants that can help contain fire rather than fuel a fire. Hardwood trees are less flammable than pine, evergreen, eucalyptus or fir trees. Firewise.org – a project and website created and maintained by the National Fire Protection Association – provides links to a number of state Cooperative Extension Service pages that feature lists of regional plants and trees that are particularly resistant to fire.

- Use fire-resistant or noncombustible materials on the roof and exterior structure of the dwelling. Treat wood or combustible material used in roofs, siding, decking, or trim with UL-approved fire-retardant chemicals.

In 2013, there were 47,579 wildfires across the U.S., burning more than 4 million acres of land. The top five states with wildfires were California, North Carolina, Georgia, Oregon and Arizona. People living in fire prone areas should be ready to evacuate in a moment's notice to a local shelter or a designated bug out location.

Winter storms - Even areas that normally have mild winters can be hit with a major snowstorm or extreme cold snaps. Winter storms can result in flooding, storm surge, high winds, closed highways, blocked roads, and downed power lines. Exposure (hypothermia), carbon monoxide poisoning, and auto accidents result in the greatest loss of life. Current climate changes are tending to exacerbate the impact of storms of all types.

In December, 2008, a major ice storm struck the Northeastern United States. 1.25 million homes and businesses went without power. In what was described at the time as "the worst storm of the decade," a state of emergency was declared in Massachusetts, New Hampshire, and parts of Maine. On January 26, 2009, a major ice storm struck Kentucky leaving over 600,000 homes and businesses without power for weeks.

More recently in mid-February 2014, an ice storm resulting from the Polar Vortex, made its way down from the arctic into the plain states, Midwest, Northeast and even the Southern parts of the U.S. Approximately 1.2 million homes and businesses (almost identical to the 2008 storm although this was across a broader area) lost power as the storm moved from the South through the Northeast. Power lines breaking under the weight of ice build-up, ice laden trees falling across power lines, and cars sliding and crashing into utility poles were the main causes for outages.

Ensure that your emergency plan considers

- the dangers of using candles with open flames during a power outage;
- emergency sanitation measures should water pipes burst resulting in loss of water pressure;
- having plenty of fluids to prevent dehydration;
- avoiding overexertion when shoveling snow which can bring on a heart attack - a major cause of death in winter;
- conserving heating fuel by keeping your home cooler than normal and temporarily closing off heat to some rooms;
- maintaining ventilation when using kerosene heaters to avoid build-up of toxic fumes; and
- driving only when absolutely necessary and in daylight hours as the roads may be cluttered with downed trees and power lines.

What is Your Safety Net?

In the "Good 'ol Days" (post-Depression), disasters were not as common nor as severe. A person's preparedness safety net was pretty much money in the bank. One merely had to work at the same job for 30-40 years, save a little money and then retire to Florida and enjoy the warm sea breezes. That dream is a lot more difficult today. Technology alone has had a tremendous effect on our lives in the past 20 years.

Many can remember getting their first cell phone that came in a shoebox size case. Then calling the corporate office and reminding someone to look at a new thing called "email" to find the weekly report. The first word processors were trained personnel who could use the system. All of which seems so yesterday! But the world is different today where

- governments around the world are paralyzed, heavy-handed and insecure;
- religion drives more wedges between people than politics;
- people have a "what's in it for me" attitude;
- society is angrier than ever before;
- transportation is costly, convenient and dangerous all at the same time;
- economies are fragile and tend to be manipulated by the wealthy;
- weather is more predictable and more destructive; and
- employers are tentative and cautious in light of all the above.

While the scale of issues facing us today is perhaps larger, the above list could have come from the 19th century as well. What does this tell us? Change is inevitable and you need to be planning on change in every element of your life including emergency preparedness.

A common theme of the unprepared is "what do I need to prepare for where I live?" People will tell you "it never floods here" or "I don't live in earthquake country." Consider the following events

- A government shutdown that could impact your income directly or indirectly. If you do not work for the government, maybe you run a small business near a military base or large government offices.
- Losing your job. Do you have marketable skills that could get you a job elsewhere? If not think about how you can make yourself more marketable in the new advent of employment. Education is rarely bad for you but advancing some technical skills could be helpful too. How much savings do you have while you look for new employment?
- Localized rioting and looting. Could you last a week or two in your home without a trip to the grocery store?
- A stock market that tumbles on global news and cuts your retirement savings in half.
- An employer that changes their retirement policy and will no longer offer you a full pension or health insurance.

- Unprecedented power outages that render ATMs and gas stations useless due to an aging power grid.
- Higher gasoline prices due to wars in the Middle East and developing nations with new found oil demand.
- A technology advancement that renders your career/industry obsolete.
- Drought that raises the cost of most farm foods and beef.
- Avian influenza that wipes out millions of chickens causing a spike in both chicken and egg prices.

This is just a small list, but given all the potential uncertainty in the world what will be your preparedness safety net?

Theoretical Disasters

In addition to the lengthy list of realistic hazards presented, there is an endless list of theoretical disasters that reality TV has us consider. However, their catastrophic occurrences have relatively low probabilities. For the most part, your emergency preparations for the more common hazards should serve you well just in case some of these theoretical disasters do come to pass:

- shifting of the poles,
- accelerated rising of sea levels,
- collapse of the dollar and financial systems,
- anarchy (domestic or global),

- civil war,
- daily terrorist attacks in U.S.,
- global drought,
- loss of fresh water sources, and
- lack of sufficient food production.

Summary

This chapter has made it clear not all potential disasters are weather dependent! Do not focus on just one disaster; think outside the box a little while you analyze potential threats to your life style. A catastrophic event like those listed herein could significantly alter your life plans and perhaps force you to change the way you live and even where you live. Why not be a little prepared just in case?

References:

1. Becky Oskin, *Man-Made Earthquakes Rising in US*, LiveScience, http://www.livescience.com/50588-hazard-maps-manmade-earthquakes.html, retrieved April 23, 2015.
2. National Fire Protection Association, *Fires in the U.S.*, http://www.nfpa.org/research/reports-and-statistics/fires-in-the-us, retrieved April 22,2015.
3. William J. Broad,*U.S. Rethinks Strategy for the Unthinkable*, New York Times, December 15, 2010.
4. Robert Walton, Utility Dive, *Why utilities are rushing to replace and modernize the aging*

grid, http://www.utilitydive.com/news/why-utilities-are-rushing-to-replace-and-modernize-the-aging-grid/361922/, February 10, 2015, Retrieved May 14, 2015.

5. United States Global Change Research Program, *Global Climate Change Impacts in the United States*, 2009.

6. Claims Journal Staff, *Army Corps of Engineers Reports Unacceptable Levees Highest in West*, http://www.claimsjournal.com/news/west/2007/02/02/76527.htm, February 2, 2007, Retrieved May 14, 2015

7. U.S Army Corps of Engineers, 2013 *National Inventory of Dams*, http://www.agc.army.mil/Media/FactSheets/FactSheetArticleView/tabid/11913/Article/480923/national-inventory-of-dams.aspx, Retrieved May 14, 2015.

8. Association of State Dam Safety Officials, *2013 Statistics on State Dam Safety Regulation*, http://www.damsafety.org/media/Documents/STATE_INFO/STATISTICS/2013_StateStats.pdf, Retrieved May 14, 2015.

9. June 2014American Society of Civil Engineers, Report Card for America's Infrastructure, Dams 2013.

10. Doyle Rice, *Is U.S. flooding getting worse?*, USA Today, May 6, 2010, http://content.usatoday.com/communities/sciencefair/post/2010/05/is-us-flooding-getting-

worse/1#.VZwSavlVhHy, Retrieved May 15, 2015.

Chapter 5 – Required Supplies

If you have learned nothing else so far remember that a disaster can happen where you live, it can happen while you are driving and it can happen sooner than you think. When it does, first responders are unlikely to be available for a couple days and disaster relief efforts take time to mobilize. This chapter is a presentation of the emergency supplies you should consider, but we will start with why you are not as prepared as you think.

Why You Are NOT as Prepared as You Think

As evidenced by several surveys since Hurricane Katrina, only around 30% of Americans say their disaster preparedness is adequate. That is a modest start given the devastation of Katrina, but of those 30%, probably about half actually have all the needed elements of a disaster plan! But let me begin with the top five reasons why you are really not as prepared for a disaster as you may think, even though you have some emergency supplies.

1. **Insufficient supplies** – Very few people seem to regularly check the contents of their emergency supplies after they buy them. Most survival food bars and water supplies have a five year shelf-life. Even though you bought some supplies five years ago, has your family changed at all since then? Do you have an infant now, small children, grown kids who have left home, or pets? Any family changes

and time could cause your emergency supplies to now be inadequate, inappropriate, or expired.

2. **Decentralized supplies** – When the contents of emergency kits are displayed at public events, folks will say, "I have one of those, and a couple of these, and some of that." But when asked where they keep all the supplies they will say "the tent is in the space over the garage with the camping gear; the first aid kit is in the bathroom; raingear is in the closet; flashlights are located in the bedroom nightstand, kitchen drawer, and garage workbench; and food is in the pantry." While it makes sense to have such items in these locations, emergencies do not allow you time to collect all of this stuff before you evacuate. Think about all of the stories you've seen on the national news about wildfire victims having only minutes to evacuate.

3. **Inadequate storage locations** – Most people have their emergency supplies at home. This is fine if your family is home during a disaster, but odds are you will be scattered around the city given your busy lifestyles. If you do not keep a car survival kit in your vehicle, you stand the chance of being stranded in your vehicle without food, water, and medical supplies. If not for a disaster, what about a single car accident on a sparsely traveled road? People read about folks getting lost or being in an accident that are stranded for days with no supplies, and many perish.

While your employer should have an emergency plan for your company, make sure you have a little something in your office just in case. Consider that for a shelter-in-place scenario at work, you may not have access to your car survival kit in the parking lot.

4. **Lack of emergency plans** – Having the right quantity of appropriate supplies in the right place is important, but so, too, is knowing how to react to various emergency scenarios that you may encounter where you live and work. You need to consider and actually document the following to complete your emergency planning.

   a. **Shelter-in-place** – how will you shelter-in-place within your home, office or car? Which room(s) is best and on which floor?

   b. **Evacuations** – how will you respond to a voluntary evacuation order? Where could you go instead of a shelter if you have the option? What emergency supplies and critical documents will you take with you and who will get what loaded in the car?

   c. **Meeting places** –where will you meet given a home emergency (i.e., fire) and where will you meet if you and your family are scattered around town at the time of an emergency?

   d. **Communications plan** – how will your family connect if they are separated during an emergency? While most anyone can tell you that phone lines and cell systems will most likely be inoperable during a major disaster, few actually consider how to check on their family members when separated. It is not uncommon to have children in two or even three different schools during the day while the parents work in different locations.

5. **Home inventory** – While few disagree that having a home inventory record is a good idea, few have actually accomplished the monumental task. It is time consuming and tedious, but extremely helpful after you have "lost everything" in a disaster. The simple way is just to take a video of every room in your home while narrating the contents as best you can. Having a record of itemized costs, especially for large ticket items, is even more helpful and can actually be used to ensure your home owners insurance is sufficient regarding replacement items.

Some folks believe if they buy a survival kit, emergency kit, go bag, bug out bag, earthquake kit, or the like; that they are prepared. Others believe you need two years' worth of food and a small arsenal to defend your food supply. On either end of the spectrum, getting dedicated supplies may be the easiest to complete, but there are other key items to consider in your family's emergency preparedness efforts to be self-sufficient in an emergency. Every emergency kit should contain your

- communication plan,

- hard or digital copies of your vital documents, and
- emergency supplies.

Emergency Supplies

SOS Emergency water pouches

Water – It is obvious from the information presented in Chapter 4 that the probability of you losing your water supply is getting higher every day. How will you and your family cope with the loss of water in your home? When the water faucets quit flowing you will not have water for

- drinking;
- mixing baby formulas;
- cooking;

- bathing, tooth brushing, and hand hygiene;
- first aid wound care;
- pets/animals drinking;
- rinsing/washing dishes;
- washing clothes;
- hot water heating;
- irrigating plants and gardens;
- ice to cool drinks and food; and
- flushing toilets.

The normal recommendation for stored water quantity is one gallon per person per day. This should be considered as the minimal amount of water you need to store. However, given any number of the items listed above, you may need significantly more than this. Carefully evaluate the individual needs of your family members to determine a sufficient amount of water to store. Keep in mind that more water the better!

How do you prepare for such inconvenience? Start by buying a little extra drinking water every week when you go to the store. Cases of plastic water bottles are the best; however, be careful where you store them as they can absorb odors from the environment making them smell or taste abnormal. Learn more about storing water.

For longer term water outages you will need much more water. Consider a 55 gallon plastic water storage barrel with siphon pump to easily access your water. You can even buy a water bladder that fits in your bathtub and can be filled with up to 100 gallons of water. However, this is really only practical when you have some advance notice of a potential water outage or shortage due to a hurricane or impending flood.

If you do not get a full water outage, but only a breach that potentially contaminates your water, you will most likely be issued a "boil water" order from your local authorities (either the water company or health agency). This type of an event will still flow water to your home for flushing your toilets but drinking the water could be hazardous. Learn more about "boil water" orders.

When water quality is in question you should also consider having some water purification drops or tablets on hand to purify questionable drinking water. Make sure you get a quality chlorine dioxide tablet that kills viruses, bacteria, and protozoa (including Giardia and Cryptosporidium). If you are at home you may have cooking containers that you can use to purify water with such tablets, otherwise make sure you have some portable plastic water bags specifically for purifying your drinking water.

Food – Non-perishable food rations are also essential for every 72 hour emergency kit. Although many people generally include a few canned goods in their kits, they are heavy, can be difficult to open, and often require water or heat for best flavor. Instead, try to include a few emergency meal packs or survival bars in your survival kit to get you by for a couple days.

Most folks understand that a three day supply should help them weather their worst emergency, until additional resources arrive. However, many hurricane victims now understand that one or two weeks' worth of emergency food supplies is a good idea. This is based upon the resulting widespread power outages and debris blocked roads that make provision replacement difficult.

Back in the booming 80's, when everyone was buying mutual funds for the future, they employed an investment technique known as "dollar cost averaging." So, while this month's shares may be cheap, next month's may be higher. But over the long run, buying a little every month provided the best average purchase price. The same goes for food products. Most folks are carefully watching for special deals on food, and when the foods you like and eat regularly go on sale, stock up. By doing so, you can slowly manage to build up your family's emergency food supply and save money too. But don't buy such foods impulsively, you need a solid strategy. The five simple steps to food storage include:

1. purchase foods you like to eat;
2. determine how much of what you like to eat is storable;
3. purchase storable foods regularly;
4. eat what you store to rotate stock; and
5. take inventory regularly, so you always know what to replace.

A real key here is "Eat what you store." Having 1000 pounds of wheat on hand is of little use, if you cannot grind it and make bread, or it is all you have stored.

Similarly, having 100 cans of Spam will not help if no one in your family will eat Spam!

Another great long-term food storage solution is freeze-dried meals that can include a variety of fruits, meals, and drinks. Several manufacturers are providing such meals that can be stored for up to 20 years! For the most part these meals require water to be added and heat to warm the foods. They are actually pretty tasty and a good value for the money. Freeze-dried meals should definitely be a component of your overall food storage plan.

If you really like your hot meals consider the modern day meals ready to eat (MRE) which are significantly improved over the WWII era military meals ready to eat. Heater Meals is a company that makes delicious entrées or complete meals that have a built-in chemical heater system and water pouch to provide you with a hot meal in minutes. With such meals you do not need any additional water or fuel for cooking and they store for up to two years.

Prescriptions – For those who require daily prescription medications to maintain their health, you must keep a supply of all your prescription medications in your emergency kit to ensure consistent medication while you are away from home. To make refilling these medications easier while away, keep a copy of the prescription or the prescription number in your kit as well.

First aid supplies – Most people have a small first aid kit in case of an emergency. They are aware of the need for various sizes of adhesive and plastic band aids, burn cream, tweezers, and the like. But there are other critical items you should include:

- **Dressings & bandages** – Bleeding is generally a number one priority in emergency medical operations. Have plenty of 4x4 dressings and roller gauze bandaging material available to make pressure bandages. One or two larger dressings (5" x 9") could also be very useful for larger lacerations or eviscerations. Remember, in a pinch, a sanitary napkin makes an excellent dressing.
- **Antiseptic wipes** – Every emergency first aid kit should also have the supplies needed to properly clean a wound, such as antiseptic wipes, and antibiotic ointment to prevent infection.
- **Disposable gloves** – The best choice for disposable gloves would be Nitrile gloves that contain no latex and are of medical examination quality. Being able to isolate yourself from various infectious or contaminated body fluids will be critical to your safety and survival in an emergency.
- **Respirators** – Having at least a few N95 respirator facemasks in your kit is a great way to stay prepared for dozens of possible emergencies such as protection from debris dust following an earthquake, or the influenza virus. Additionally, you

could have some Air-Aid Emergency
Masks that have both bacterial and
activated carbon filter stages. These are
effective in protecting against: pepper
spray and teargas agents, Anthrax, Hanta
virus, biological agents, radioactive
materials, smoke, toxic chemicals, and
communicable diseases.

- **Instant cold packs** – An instant ice pack
  is a great addition to any emergency first
  aid kit. These packs can be activated by
  simply squeezing and shaking to generate
  up to 30 minutes of icy pain relief. No
  refrigerated storage required.

- **Splinting materials** – While you can
  never be sure of the extent of a
  musculoskeletal injury, having a splint to
  immobilize a broken leg, sprained ankle,
  or strained elbow is good. Considering it
  may be a while before you can get a
  victim with such injuries to a doctor, being
  able to effectively immobilize the injury
  and reduce swelling could be critical.
  Splints manufactured by SAM Medical
  Products (or SAM splints) are compact,
  lightweight, and come with various
  splinting option pictures to assist in
  treatment.

- **Triangular bandages** – These are a
  natural, woven cotton muslin gauze
  bandage (40" x 40" x 56"). They make an
  excellent all-purpose sling for
  immobilizing injured arms, wrists and

shoulders. Two bandages are needed in order to make a sling and swathe for increased injury stabilization.

- **Eye wash** – You should always have a bottle of eye wash in your emergency first aid kit to safely remove foreign materials from the eyes; or to relieve itching or burning due to smoke or air pollutants. The last place you want to be is in an emergency with a loss of eye sight.

- **CPR breathing mask** – In order to provide good quality rescue breaths for an individual that is not breathing or during CPR, this mask with a one-way valve will protect you from direct contact with a victim.

- **Emergency blankets** – These traditional mylar blankets are extremely compact and are capable of retaining up to 90% of your body heat. These have various uses including hypothermia recovery and the prevention of shock.

Lighting devices –You should always have multiple light sources in your survival kit (e.g., flashlight, head light and Cyalume light sticks). Consider flashlights that can be shaken or wound up and do not require batteries. When possible, only select lights that require the same battery size to prevent having multiple sizes of backup batteries. Such lighting devices can also be used to alert rescuers to your location.

Portable radio – Regardless of the disaster and whether you are sheltering-in-place or evacuating, you will want to get constant updated event information from the Emergency Alert System. Your best choice may be a hand-crank or solar powered radio. Some units actually provide hand-crank, solar, and DC power options. Again, if you can eliminate batteries from your kit you will reduce your kit maintenance requirements.

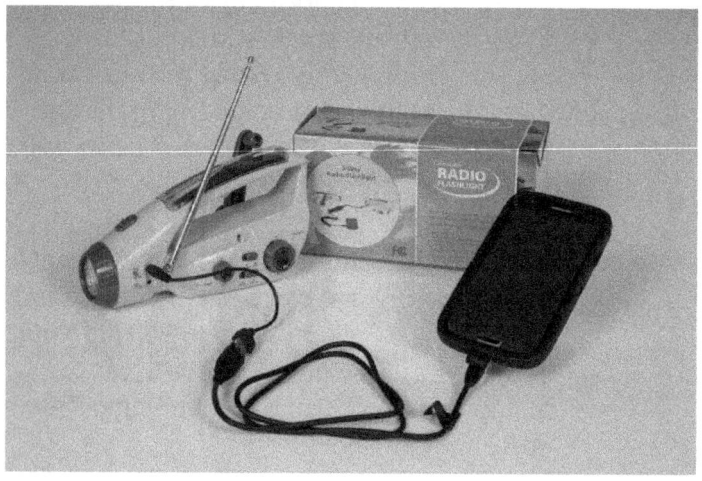

Portable AM/FM Radio/Flashlight

Sanitation items – When your water is off, your toilets can not flush. How will you handle sanitation for three days without a water supply? Many home emergency kits that come in five gallon plastic containers can be used as a toilet with the included toilet seat and bags. In an emergency situation, or natural disaster, sanitation will become a serious issue. Following most such events, the single largest concern is the outbreak of various diseases spawned by improper or lax sanitation practices. Since you might be without water from mere hours or even days, it is important to add items like hand sanitizer or sanitary wipes to your 72 hour emergency kit.

Shelter items – You should always consider some emergency shelter items like a tarp, tube tent, or an emergency privacy shelter. It is also a good idea to keep a sleeping bag or thermal blankets with your shelter supplies so that you can stay warm during a cold night. If you live in a very cold climate, you might also want to invest in some hand and body warming packs.

Communication items – It is recommended that you have at least one corded telephone (landline) that is not dependent on electricity in case of an electrical power outage. Most cordless telephones usually have receivers that are electrically charged and will not work during a power outage. Many phones now have batteries inside to allow them to work for some time should a power outage occur. These batteries need to be refreshed regularly similar to your smoke detectors. Another good reason to maintain a landline telephone is to facilitate communication between emergency planners and your home via reverse 911 systems where implemented. Using such a system, emergency planners can record an evacuation or shelter-in-place message to be delivered to thousands of homes per minute. Many such systems are capable of geographically targeting homes via a city or county GIS (Geographical Information System). Using this technology, it is possible to isolate the reverse 911 messages to specific neighborhoods or streets.

You can also use your landline home phone to communicate with family and friends by using the voice mail feature (generally available at an additional cost). With this you can leave and retrieve message remotely through a cell phone. It is critical however, to know how to access your home voice mail remotely via your cell phone. During an emergency is no time to try and figure this process out, especially considering you will not have access to your owner's manual.

Because most people have a cell phone, here are some tips for using your cell phone in an emergency:

- make sure you program all of your emergency contact numbers into your cell phone (e.g., local police department, fire station, power company(s), insurance providers, local hospital(s), all family members and your emergency out-of-state contact);
- ensure your friends, neighbors, and family know your cell phone number as well;
- keep your wireless phone batteries charged at all times;
- have an alternate plan to recharge your phone battery in case of power outages (i.e. charging via your DC car charger, extra cell phone battery, hand crank generator, or solar device with appropriate adapters);
- keep your phone dry and out of environments with excessive humidity;
- forward your home phone to your cell phone number in the event of an evacuation (call forwarding is based out of the telephone

central office, so you will get incoming calls from your landline phone, even if your local telephone service is disrupted at your home);

- use your wireless phone to access local weather information via a phone service or the Internet (if your phone is so configured);
- if you have a camera phone, you can take, store, and send photos of damaged property to your insurance company from your phone (make sure your phone service plan covers this and practice before you need to send photos);
- make sure your service plan covers text messaging (text messages will often go through quicker than voice calls and again know how to send a text message before you need to);
- more importantly, text messaging frees up voice lines for emergency personnel; and
- when redialing with your cell phone, wait 10 seconds between redial attempts so the data sent from your phone to the cell sites has enough time to clear before you resend the same data.

In addition to your telephonic communication devices, consider also an AM/FM radio that can run without electricity. Such access during a power failure will keep you in touch with the emergency alert system. Another good option would be a National Oceanic and Atmospheric Administration (NOAA) radio that is a nationwide network of radio stations broadcasting continuous weather information directly from the nearest National Weather Service office. The radios broadcast official Weather Service warnings, watches, forecasts and other hazard information 24 hours a day, seven days a week.

The final communication devise accessible to most people could be a HAM radio. While other forms of communication were not working after Hurricane Katrina, HAM radio operators were able to communicate and identify areas of need for first responders. While technically anyone can operate a HAM radio during an actual emergency, normal communication via HAM requires at least a Technician license that can be acquired by contacting the local HAM radio club in your area.

Comfort supplies – Once you have collected all the essential emergency items you may consider the following comfort supplies which will make the emergency a little more tolerable:

- emergency cash (the amount is the amount you need to feel comfortable with for three to seven days of expenses);
- over-the-counter (OTC) medications (e.g., aspirin, non-aspirin, anti- diarrheal, etc.);
- personal items (e.g., glasses, hearing aid batteries, contact lens solution, spare contacts, etc.); and
- personal hygiene supplies.

Nice to have . . .hard to carry supplies – Many people consider the following items when evacuating; however, this significantly complicates the evacuation. In simple terms it is a lot of stuff that requires a lot of room which you may not have in your evacuation vehicle. Another reason to seriously question the need for these supplies is that there is little room for all this in an evacuation center if that is where you are headed. However, if you have made plans to go and stay with relatives until the disaster is mitigated and you can return home, some of these items may make sense to pack in your evacuation vehicle:

- one gallon of water/day/person,
- cooking utensils,
- clothing (seasonally adjusted),
- bedding (e.g., pillows, blankets).

More complicated supplies – Most emergency kit recommendations are for "normal" families. Should you have family members with special needs (e.g., communication, hearing, mobility, mental, or visual), or pets or livestock, your supply list must expand to accommodate their needs.

- Consider the following for family members with special needs:
  - refrigerated medications, and
  - support devices (e.g., hearing aids, batteries, cane, wheelchair, scooter, written instructions, oxygen, catheters, etc.).
- For your pets/animals remember
  - food and water to last the duration of the evacuation,

- veterinary records (i.e., specifically immunizations),
- proper identification (i.e., local licenses when required).
- pet carrier and/or leash, and
- livestock will generally require a trailer for transport, and more food and water).

Maintenance of supplies – After expending the effort to assemble your dedicated emergency supplies, it is critical to maintain the supplies. To prevent the expiration, deterioration or usefulness of your supplies, you should check them out twice a year. Two good times are when daylight savings time starts and stops and you change the batteries in your smoke/carbon monoxide detectors. The following events will trigger maintenance activities.

- **Family changes** – Anytime new family members arrive, you will need to add supplies to your kits. Similarly, as children age and leave the house, you may be able to reduce the amount of supplies needed based on family size.
- **Health changes** – As we age, we tend to require more medications for both preventative and remedial purposes. Any changes in long-term health and associated prescriptions/OTC medications need to be accounted for in your supplies.
  Given that most prescriptions generally only provide a maximum of 90 days' worth of the medication you will need to constantly replace

your emergency supply with "fresh" medications. If you keep a weeks' worth of your medications in your emergency kit, every time you fill a new prescription, use the older medications in your kit and replace them with your new prescription.

- **Expiration** – Food, packaged water, and medications all have expiration dates. Most emergency food bars and water pouches have a maximum shelf-life of five years. While water never really goes bad, it can become stale and take on odors from the surrounding environment such as gasoline and oils in a garage. Keeping the water fresh will keep the taste palatable.

Should any of your supplies require batteries to operate, those batteries also have "best used by" dates. To maximize the usefulness of your supplies, ensure that any items that require batteries all use the same size batteries. This prevents you from having to maintain an inventory of multiple battery sizes.

Water purification tablets and liquid purification drops also have expiration dates that must be checked. Certain medications in standard first aid kits such as Ibuprofen, aspirin, non-aspirin, triple antibiotic ointment, and eye wash generally have expiration dates as well.

While many of your supplies may contain plastic, consideration needs to be given for storing items in hot areas which can degrade such components. Similarly, first aid kits may contain basic medications (e.g., eye wash and antibiotic ointments) that have expiration dates, and storage in hot environments (e.g., garages, car trunks, etc.) may cause adhesive band aids and other supplies to "melt" together and become useless.

- **Environment changes** – Another important reason to maintain your supplies is based on environmental changes. When moving from a warm to colder climate, you may need to consider adding items to provide warmth (e.g., hand warmers, stocking caps, gloves, etc.). Similarly, if you are lucky enough to be moving from a cold climate to a warmer one, you may be able to remove some cold weather items and replace them with sunglasses and flip flops.

- **Seasonal changes** – Finally, every six months you should be able to align your supplies with the upcoming seasons. In March or April when daylight savings time starts, consider removing your cold weather items to simplify and reduce the amount of supplies you have in your kits. Conversely, in October or November when daylight savings time ends, make sure your cold weather gear is appropriately staged in your kits. For those living in states that do not recognize daylight savings time, review your gear when everyone else changes their clocks.

While this can all seem daunting, remember not every supply requirement applies to you.

Go Bags

Have you ever seen people on TV being interviewed after evacuating their home in the middle of an oncoming wildfire? They are often complaining that they had no idea what to take with them with only minutes to evacuate under a police order. They grabbed a couple family photo albums and ran. Sadly, it happens more often than not!

In general terms, one would need to evacuate their home or office given an impending hurricane, wildfire or flood, all of which usually provide some advance warning. Once in a while, it may be necessary based upon a hazardous material (HAZMAT) event or an imminent HAZMAT event (e.g., a burning propane tank car on the tracks through your neighborhood that could explode).

The purpose of a "Go Bag" is to contain those critical items you may need when you have to evacuate your home. Such bags are best assembled in one container and easy to grab on the way out of your house. The concept here is not to "include the kitchen sink" but rather include the "must have" items. Go bags should also be in a backpack as this allows you to keep both hands free to manage children or negotiate debris during evacuations.

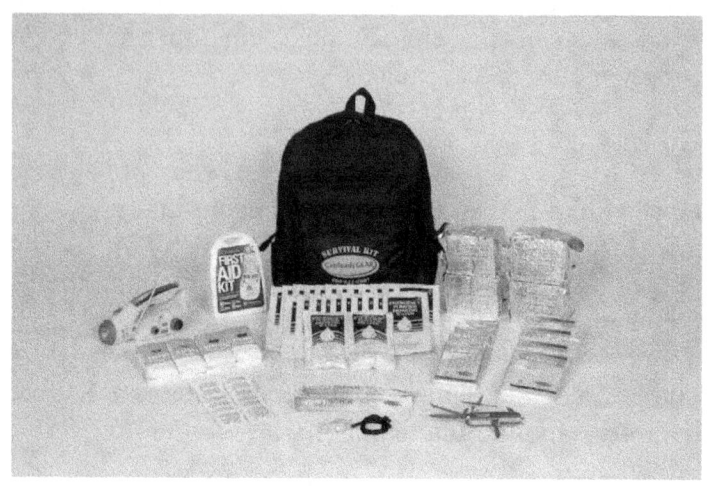

Premium 4 Person Go Bag

The contents of your go bag (each family member of appropriate age should have one) will depend upon the following factors:

- Where you evacuate.
- When you evacuate.
- How you will evacuate.
- Duration of evacuation.

Where – If you are heading to an organized Red Cross shelter, you will not need sleeping cots or bedding material, and food and water will be available. However, you might think about including a small amount of water, snacks, and personal hygiene items in your go bag in case it takes a while to complete food preparation at the shelter. Remember, "You really don't want to be number 10,001 in line for a bottle of water." Similarly, if you are able to evacuate to a friend's or relative's house, you could get by with minimal supplies. But remember, it is important to know in advance if your friend or relative has adequate sleeping accommodations, linens, and food, to support your stay.

If you are evacuating to a "secure" or "hide-away" location known only to your family, you may require additional supplies depending upon the amount of supplies stored at such a location. You may need more food, water, and shelter items if the location has no cache of usable supplies. Care must always be taken to ensure that any caches of long-term stored supplies are fresh and not expired.

When – Depending upon where you live, the time of year you are evacuating can affect the contents of your go bag. Obviously the greatest differences occur between summer and winter with the potential for extreme hot and cold environments. Go bags should be modified when cold weather gear (e.g., gloves, stocking caps, etc.) are no longer required. However, you could be forced to evacuate at night which in some locales might require additional warm clothing or thermal blankets and chemical warming pads.

How – If you are evacuating on foot, the weight of your go bag should be an obvious consideration. Most folks are not used to carrying a heavy backpack. Walking two miles for exercise is one thing but walking two miles with a 20 pound backpack is something else! Think critical items only and in sufficient quantities to get you to your destination without too many extras.

If you can evacuate by car, you have many more options and can certainly take more items when you go. The trick here is to make sure you have pre-staged go bags and a list of additional items that you may be able to load in your vehicle if you have the time and depending upon your destination. This list could include items such as blankets, pillows, additional clothing, and food items. The list could also include family heirlooms and other valuable items (e.g., guns, coins, cash, jewelry, etc.). Just remember that your vehicle may be parked in a less than secure area where vehicle thefts could occur.

Duration – Most emergency evacuations range from a couple of hours to a couple of weeks as with larger events such as hurricanes. Depending upon your local weather and environment, you need to plan for realistic evacuation scenarios. Why plan on a two to three month evacuation due to coastal flooding if you live in Indiana? Do not plan for a wildfire evacuation if you live in a big metropolitan city. Key items that are dependent upon the duration of your evacuation include food, water, hygiene products, medications, and sanitation supplies.

Remember you can go crazy adding stuff to a go bag depending on the potential for emergencies and the environment you live in, but can you carry it on foot? Carefully consider all items you include in your go bags. Make arrangements for possible evacuation places well ahead of time and consider evacuating BEFORE it is mandatory, and you will have a much better time compared to people who wait until everyone else is leaving and get stuck in traffic with supply shortages. Do not feel pressured to get all the supplies at once, it is important for you to put together your go bags as soon as realistically feasible but you can do it in phases to spread out the costs.

Other critical supplies

Fuel storage for emergencies

Fuel – As we learned from Hurricane Sandy (2012), not only does strong wind cause damage, but the storm surge can be devastating during a hurricane. The record storm surge experienced during this event made visible the fragility of New York Harbor's fuel supply chain. The ability to move gasoline and other fuels around the Northeast was truncated at almost every link:

- Oil tankers were unable to move into port and off-load new crude supplies because of the debris that filled the harbor.
- Refineries in low lying areas were flooded and forced to shut down.
- Pipelines stopped flowing and storage depots could not move fuel because of power outages.
- Commercial tanker trucks were delayed getting to local gas stations as they were being commandeered by emergency agencies.
- Two-thirds of local gas stations could not pump fuel due to power outages.

Aside from the occasional "superstorm" there is one more thing those in the Northeast need to start worrying about – the refineries that make gasoline, diesel, and heating oil are closing at an alarming rate. In general, refineries currently operating in the United States are 30 to 50+ years old. These older eastern refineries are simply losing so much money that their owners are selling them or closing them down. Most recently shuttered refineries include

- Sunoco's Eagle Point Refinery, Westville, NJ, closed in 2010.[1]
- Sunoco's Marcus Hook Refinery, Marcus Hook, PA, closed in late 2011[2] and is being retrofitted as a natural gas liquids storage and distribution complex.
- Western Refining's Yorktown Refinery, Yorktown, VA, closed in late 2010[3] and has

been converted to a transportation terminal for fuels.

- Hovensa's St. Croix, U.S. Virgin Islands refinery (one of the world's largest oil refineries) closed in early 2012.
- Additionally, several European refineries, another source for gasoline in the U.S., have recently closed down or are up for sale.

Our existing refinery sites are concentrated in coastal areas and are susceptible to natural disasters. Nearly 30% of the U.S. refining capacity was threatened by Hurricane Rita (2005). Similar threats were imposed by Hurricane Katrina later in 2005. On the production side, consider the upstream impact of shutting down all the oil rigs in the Gulf of Mexico that produce the crude to refine as well!

But aside from the Northeast, refineries around the country continue to demonstrate problems associated with aging equipment and natural disasters. Four workers were killed and three others critically burned in late March 2013 when an explosion tore through a Tesoro oil refinery in Anacortes, Washington. Citgo Petroleum Corp. said its Lemont refinery in Illinois was able to remain operational on May 2, 2013 despite minor flooding and electrical issues caused by extreme weather conditions. The ExxonMobil refinery in Torrance, CA had an explosion in February 2015.

When updating your disaster preparedness plans, you need to consider that gasoline may not be available post disaster down at the corner station. Flooding or earthquake damage may prevent tankers from getting to your area. Power outages could prevent stations from pumping any gasoline they do have in their tanks. There could be widespread gasoline rationing imposed by the government! Plan ahead and consider the following preps:

- safely store some emergency gasoline at home (flammable material storage containers recommended);
- keep your vehicle(s) as full of gasoline as possible (given today's fluctuating gas prices, filling up more often may allow you to dollar-cost-average your fuel purchases);
- work with neighbors if possible to ensure additional fuel supplies;
- never head out driving in hopes of finding gasoline somewhere, as you will most likely run out and be stranded;
- use your most fuel efficient vehicle when evacuating; or
- learn how to safely siphon gasoline from one of your vehicles to another.

Generator – Depending upon the extent of the disaster and resulting power outage you may want to consider a small portable generator that could at least keep your refrigerator and freezer running along with a light or two in the house. When looking at generators consider those that can run on gasoline or propane which provides more flexibility depending upon fuel availability post disaster. Size is also another consideration as the unit will need to be stored somewhere. Some of the small 2000Kw Honda generators are the size of a small suitcase.

Solar charger – Perhaps in lieu of a generator to run key appliances you may just want to have a small solar charger unit that can keep your cell phone, tablet or laptop charged so you can continue to stay informed about the unfolding disaster. Larger commercial solar systems could keep your appliances and lights on during a power outage; however, these are expensive.

Summary

What do you need to survive comfortably? Everyone has a different answer for this and it is very individualized. Where will you go if evacuated? Consider several options here and identify any special supplies you may need given your actual evacuation scenario. What about your pets? Do you have enough cash if ATMs are inoperable? Take the time to consider your actions and options and include the whole family in the discussion. Remember the object here is not to alarm family members, but to remind them that contingency planning for the worse is always a smart idea.

Start assembling the critical supplies you may need to survive the worse possible scenario in your neighborhood, city, county or state. Remember you don't need to go to extremes here, just do some prudent planning and emergency preparedness, so you and your family can be self-sufficient for at least three days should the worse ever happen to you.

If you are looking for a significant return on your investment, try building up your emergency supplies and enjoy the peace of mind of preparedness! If you follow the middle ground prepping approach in this book you do not need to spend extravagantly to prepare your family. Just do a little something to start and you will be well on your way. It is the same process as saving more money each month, losing weight, or getting in shape at the gym, you just have to start small. You can call it prepping if you like, but you need to *prepare for the unexpected*®.

References:

1. Bryan Littel, *Sunoco Demolishing Eagle Point Refinery*, West Deptford Patch, http://patch.com/new-jersey/westdeptford/sunoco-demolishing-eagle-point-refinery, February 18, 2012. Retrieved May 7, 2015.
2. Kathleen E. Carey, Daily Times News, *Sunset? Sunoco idles Marcus Hook refinery; lays off 490 workers*, http://www.delcotimes.com/general-news/20111202/sun-set-sunoco-idles-marcus-hook-refinery-lays-off-490-workers, December 2, 2011. Retrieved May 7, 2015.
3. Amanda Kerr, *Former refinery reshaped as a transportation terminal*, Daily Press, http://articles.dailypress.com/2012-06-19/news/dp-nws-york-pipeline-terminal-0614-20120619_1_yorktown-refinery-western-refining-crude-oil, June 19, 2012. Retrieved May 7, 215

4. Associated Press business staff, *Major oil refinery to close in U.S. Virgin Islands*, American Press, http://www.cleveland.com/business/index.ssf/2012/01/major_oil_refinery_to_close_in.html, January 18, 2012, Retrieved May 7, 2015.

Chapter 6 – Middle Ground Prepping

Fissures create middle ground as a result of an earthquake

In the TV series "Doomsday Preppers, Bugged Out" and "Doomsday Preppers" there was a definite focus on extreme preparedness efforts. While the motivations and preparations are interesting and educational, how many of us live on 20 acres, have hundreds of thousands of dollars to spend on prepping structures and supplies, and have a bug-out cabin in the woods?

On the other end of the prepping spectrum are the millions of Americans who have done nothing to assemble some form of emergency supplies to support themselves in case of local civil unrest, economic collapse or regional weather disasters.

Their plan must be to depend on the generosity of the rest of you to support the Red Cross (with cash donations) and FEMA (with your tax donations).

Somewhere in between fanatical doomsday prepping and those with nothing lies what I refer to as "middle ground prepping." Middle ground prepping is a concept that provides a measured and reasonable response to preparing for impending emergencies or disasters in order to protect yourself and your family.

Basically, prepping needs to be considered as just another form of insurance like health, life, and auto. Currently, many states have mandated auto insurance and drivers can be fined if found driving without proof of insurance. The country now has mandated health insurance and can fine citizens who have no coverage. However, what if the government mandated the type and amount of preparedness supplies each person must have stocked away for an emergency?

In Chapter 2 we identified many instances of government run programs that have a history of inefficiency. What if the Legislature decided to underfund FEMA's emergency operation efforts in an attempt to force the public to take on more preparedness responsibility? Imagine how well this might be crafted by our legislators and run by our federal bureaucracy? If you have inadequate or no supplies might you be fined? If you have too many pounds of rice stored away, would you have to give it to someone who has less? Not unlike some legislative plans to remove excess guns from legal gun owners around the country. Now some will say this is a far-fetched notion, while others will say, "I never thought of it that way." But rather than dive off the deep end into an abyss of preparedness tasks, let's opt for middle ground prepping!

Remember to approach middle ground prepping as you would any project, a little at a time. This has less impact on your budget and allows you to slowly grow your preparation capabilities. Don't get caught up in the drama of reality television, thinking that you must prepare for Armageddon. It is unlikely that you will be the sole person responsible for re-growing supersteak tomatoes or repopulating the world. Remember, middle ground prepping is NOT doomsday prepping.

In Chapter 5 we identified the fact that the majority of Americans have no emergency preparedness supplies or plans. Of the 30% that admit to having some supplies, many of those may have inadequate supplies or plans:

- insufficient supplies,
- decentralized supplies,
- inadequate locations,
- lack of emergency plans, and
- lack of a home inventory.

In this chapter we will provide a road map and helpful tips for getting prepared and overcoming these typical inadequacies. This will be done using the reasonable and prudent concept of middle ground prepping in five simple steps:

- planning,
- acquiring,
- responding,
- training, and
- evaluating.

Planning

You never know when an emergency or disaster will strike, and you never know if you will be forced to stay within or evacuate your home at a moment's notice. To protect your family, the best defense against an emergency is proper preparation. To simplify your emergency planning process and break it down into smaller manageable tasks, the following guide is presented in order of importance.

1. **Identifying potential risks** – A key component of your situational awareness and your emergency plan is the analysis of hazards you could face daily in your locale. Keep in mind that your locale includes where you live, where you work, where you shop, and your children's schools.

   Initially, hazard assessments were used to evaluate a work place, or work situation, for potential hazards that employees may encounter while performing their job. However, in the early 80's FEMA adapted a hazard assessment methodology to assist states and local entities in evaluating and prioritizing potential hazards in their region. Hazard mitigation requirements for State governments started in 1994, with the Sec. 409 Hazard Mitigation Plan from States. The

Disaster Mitigation Act (DMA) of 2000 mandated mitigation plans by both state and local governments, and those plans are required to have a risk assessment component.

The good news is you do not need to actually conduct your own hazard assessment; you can leverage all the good work done by either your state or local government! Statewide Emergency Management Agencies, counties, and cities generally have such assessment information in their Emergency Operations Plans. These plans consider natural, technological, and man-made hazards. The Hazards Assessment considers two key components, vulnerability and probability. Vulnerability is the percentage of population and property likely to be affected under an "average" occurrence of the hazard. Probability is the likelihood of the future occurrence of the hazard within a specified period of time. This provides the jurisdiction with a sense of hazard priorities, or relative risk. This assessment does not predict the occurrence of a particular hazard, but it does "quantify" the risk of one hazard compared with another. By doing this analysis, planning can first be focused where the risk is greatest. In other words, there is no need to plan for a volcanic eruption in Florida, or a tsunami in Indiana. Hazard considerations usually include

- **Natural hazards** – Most jurisdictions should assess earthquakes, fires (especially wildland-urban interface), floods, landslides and debris flows, snow/ice/extreme cold, and windstorms (i.e., hurricanes, tornadoes). Where it applies, jurisdictions should also assess for coastal erosion, sea level increases, drought, tsunamis, dust storms, El Niño – La Niña weather patterns, tornadoes, and volcanic hazards.

- **Technological hazards** – Jurisdictions may assess dam failures; hazardous material accidents (both at a fixed site and via transportation routes); SCADA (Supervisory Control and Data Acquisition) system failures at processing facilities (e.g., waste water, refineries, chemical plants, electrical grids, etc.); loss of Internet or communication systems; and possibly radiological hazards.
- **Man-made hazards** – Jurisdictions also will consider certain man-made hazards. These would include acts of terrorism, civil disobedience (rioting), and active shooter events.
- **Other hazards** – Some hazards that have low probability factors may not be included in jurisdictional assessments. This could include solar flares (and resulting EMPs), collapse of the monetary system, and nuclear war.

To access your local jurisdiction's hazard assessment or emergency plan simply do a web search. Most entities have their plans available online for constituent review. You can start with the State Emergency Management Agency web sites for hazards information in your state. Then look at your local county or city websites for hazard assessments or emergency plans. With this information, you can intelligently refine your own personal emergency plans for the most probable events in your area.

2. **Emergency escape routes** – One of the most important factors of a good emergency plan are well thought out and efficient emergency escape and evacuation routes. These should be considered for both your home and your neighborhood/city.

   First, you should have two escape routes identified for each room in your house. Draw out a simple map of each floor of the home, mark doorways and windows, and designate escape routes with large arrows. Keep in mind that some emergencies, such as a house fire, could render one escape route unavailable. This is why it is critical to ensure that all family members of appropriate age know about alternate escape routes so they do not become trapped in a house fire. If you have a second floor on your house, having an easily accessible portable escape ladder in each upstairs bedroom is also a good idea.

   Once you have identified all the potential escape routes walk around your home's exterior make sure there are no obstacles in the way of those escape routes. This may include obstacles such as rose bushes outside a window, a patio cover or fence under a second story window, or an air conditioning unit. Make sure each member of the family understands it is never safe to re-enter the home after a disaster until it is deemed safe by the proper authorities.

Secondly, in regards to evacuating your neighborhood or even city, you need to make sure you have good situational awareness of all potential evacuation routes. Keep in mind, that depending upon the situation; you will never know exactly which way to evacuate from your city. However, your local emergency operations center or emergency management agency should have a good idea of the scope and extent of the looming disaster and will be broadcasting viable evacuation routes over the emergency alert system. Do not make the mistake of heading out on your favorite route as it may be congested with downed power lines, vehicle accidents, or roadway damage. Make sure that you document (in general terms) all of your potential evacuation routes (e.g., take Main Street east to the freeway, or take Interstate 80 west or take Highway 160 south).

The other critical consideration regarding evacuation routes is that you may not be home when an evacuation is ordered; such as work or school. It is essential that those who drive are aware of how to get from work or school to potential evacuation routes. Also, depending upon the nature of the evacuation and if you do not have a vehicle; think about alternate transportation methods such as a bus, train, or intra-city light rail if they are still running. Since you may not regularly use these transportation options it would be a good exercise for family members to take a short trip via each potential mode to ensure they know how to buy a ticket, or pay for, and access each mode.

3. **Meeting places** – Once you have figured out your escape and potential evacuation routes, it is time to figure out how your family members will meet up after escaping your house or a larger area evacuation. Your first meeting place should be somewhere close to your house such as a neighbor's house or maybe a community mailbox in your neighborhood. It is here, after escaping a home fire, burglary or other emergency that family members will immediately go after escaping. It will be here that you can take a head count and ensure all family members are safely out of the house. While meeting in your front or back yard could be considered, your preferred location should be clear of any first responders who arrive on the scene. If you whole family is standing on the front lawn during a house fire, you could be in the way of firefighters laying hose to your house. It is also good to document a secondary meeting place nearby for situations where being too near the house is not a good idea as in the case of energized electrical lines that are down on the ground. The number one objective should be for each member to escape by the safest means possible, and then meet up with the family at your predetermined meeting location(s).

The second meeting place you need to consider is a primary and secondary place to meet farther away from your home if you need to evacuate your community in an emergency. This option may take a little more planning as you must consider that your family may be scattered around town when disaster strikes. For example, Dad may be working downtown, Mom working in the suburbs, one child is at the local high school and another child is at the local middle school. In such a situation, where is a good (or optimum) place for all four of you to meet away from your house?

First of all consider what mode of transportation is available to each family member. Mom and Dad probably have a car, but one may have taken mass transit to work. The child in high school may not be driving yet and the one in middle school may take a school bus. Assuming that the schools are not sheltering students on campus how far could they walk or where would busses take them? For this you will need to contact the school(s) to understand their emergency plan. For younger age school children, you should have an emergency contact authorized to pick up your child when you are unable to get to that school location. Remember, that emergency contact will need to know your family meeting places as well so they can get your child to you.

Given that you need to evacuate your neighborhood, you will need location(s) away from your neighborhood but are not too far for your children to potentially walk. Consider public places such as a shopping mall, restaurant, or church in which all family members have familiarity. Part of your determination may be the fact that local bus lines go right by these locations, which could expedite your family's arrival. Take your time here and make sure you use a local map to determine the optimum locations for your family to meet. Remember, every year as children change schools or you change jobs re-evaluate the appropriateness of your meeting places.

4. **Communication plan** – Your family communication plan is what will keep your family in contact during and after emergencies or severe weather events. From this communication plan you can create simple contact cards for each family member old enough to use a phone. These cards would contain emergency contact numbers and should be kept handy in a wallet, purse, briefcase, backpack, or book bag. While these contact numbers could be stored in cell phones, if you lose your phone or the battery dies, having the contact card would be essential.

In some cases, it may not be possible for your family to meet up at one location. For these cases it is important that you identify an emergency contact and make sure each family member has their phone number (on contact card) in case of an emergency. This primary contact could be local or even an in-state contact.

However, during natural disasters, such as earthquakes, hurricanes or flooding, telephone services can be interrupted for extended periods of time because of high winds, flooding, or cell tower damage. During an emergency, a great many people are trying to use their phones at the same time compared to normal call volume. When more people try to call at the same time, the increased call volume may create network congestion leading to "fast busy" signals or slow dial tone. You may also receive a message that says, "Your call cannot be completed at this time." As a result, you should also have one out-of-state emergency contact where phone service may still be available.

In selecting such an out-of-state contact, take their location into account as well. For example, consider a hurricane approaching the east coast. If you live in South Carolina and your uncle lives in North Carolina, he may not be the best out-of-state contact given that both states could be affected by the hurricane. Look for a contact far away from the anticipated hazards in your region. Once you have decided upon an appropriate out-of-state contact, make sure that you let them know that you will be using them as your emergency contact. Conversely, you could be their out-of-state emergency contact, too.

Having personally given emergency preparedness presentations for thousands there is one key flaw in the government's desire for everyone to have an out-of-state emergency contact . . . most people do not exactly know how to use that contact! The idea of such a contact is for you to be able to communicate with your immediate family through an intermediary or your out-of-state contact.

Let me present an example of how this should work. In an emergency your family of four is separated and cannot make it to either of your designated emergency meeting places. All four of you are concerned about each other and your attempts to make contact via cell phone or texting has been in vain. When this happens, try and call or text your out-of-state emergency contact. Unless the disaster is very large you have a much better chance of reaching them on your cell phone. Once you connect to your out-of-state contact, simply let them know your location and condition. If the contact has already heard from the father they can also let you know that Dad is still at work and is fine. This process is repeated for each family member that calls in and after a series of calls; the entire family should know the location and condition of all other family members.

For larger families it is suggested that each family member have a specific time to call the out-of-state contact so everyone is not trying to call at once. For example, Dad might call at five minutes past the hour, Mom would call at 10 minutes past the hour and so on until all family members have a designated call time. The following hour when Dad calls the out-of-state contact again, he should get information about all the family members that have called the contact.

Additionally, make sure that family members know how to use text messaging (also known as SMS or Short Message Service) which can often get around network disruptions when a phone call might not be able to get through. Keep texts brief and avoid long explanations.

You can also consider subscribing to alert services. Many communities now have systems that will send instant text alerts or e-mails to let you know about bad weather, road closings, local emergencies, etc. Sign up by visiting your local Office of Emergency Management web site. Many local TV stations also have weather alert applications (apps) that can provide up to the minute weather and emergency event reporting. Residents can also sign up at Nixle.com for local emergency alerts specific to your zip code.

Fight the urge to contact everyone you know during an emergency. Every additional phone call puts a strain on the local phone system. Only make critical calls and keep them short. This will help keep the system accessible to emergency personnel and first responders if needed.

One final element of your communication plan should be to find like-minded neighbors with whom you can work with in an emergency or post disaster. With a close knit group of like-minded middle ground preppers the group would be able to leverage all of their skills and resources for the good of the group.

Preparedness plans needed for best friends too

5. **Pet/Animal considerations** – For many folks, your pets are your family too. Unfortunately, many people forget the inherent difficulty of evacuating with their pets when creating a family emergency plan. First, many disasters such as thunder and lightning storms, flying debris from a hurricane, or rising flood waters will scare animals; causing them to run looking for a safe place to hide. It is important to always have a collar with identification information on your pet to facilitate the return of lost pets. For those that can afford it, micro-chipping your pet is another great way to assist in their return should they get lost.

   Second, where will you be able to go? Most emergency shelters for people do not allow animals, so you may need to find a temporary place for them to stay or board them somewhere outside the evacuation zone. Many local animal rescue organizations work closely with local emergency planners in order to establish emergency shelters near human shelters. However, you will need to provide vaccination information for your pet(s); otherwise they may be quarantined in such facilities. The good news is, people that volunteer with animal rescue organizations love animals and will take very good care of your pet.

If you are foregoing the shelter option and decide instead to evacuate to a relative's or friend's house, make sure they are aware of your pet and have the means to shelter your pet. Some housing options such as apartments, condominiums and mobile home parks have restrictions on the size of animals that can reside there while others do not permit animals. Similarly, if your evacuation plan involves heading to a hotel for a couple days make sure you know which hotels can accommodate pets.

If you have large animals or livestock that will significantly complicate evacuation. Typically, you will need some sort of trailer to safely move them. You may also need halters, lead ropes, extra feed and water, and a plan for safely collecting manure.

Remember, DO NOT CUT ANIMALS LOOSE during a disaster. Domesticated animals do not know how to "save themselves." They may continue to run succumbing to heat exhaustion in their panic. Others may stay put in familiar surroundings until it is too late.

6. **Emergency supplies** – We've all seen the Red Cross show up with hot meals and shelters for those displaced during an emergency or after a local disaster, but what if they cannot get to you or you can't get to a shelter? Consider the flooding in Colorado (September 2103) where roads were washed out and access to remote areas was only possible by helicopter. During Hurricane Katrina (2005), many areas were extremely isolated due to widespread flooding; making rescue and relief efforts difficult to impossible. The supplies you should collect and the plans you make should ensure that you and your family have some additional level of comfort and peace-of-mind in the event of a disaster or emergency situation. Again, do you really want to be number 10,001 in line for a bottle of water or a meal at a Red Cross shelter? We all need some form of emergency supplies with us at all times in our car, at the office, and at home.

While true survivalists require top of the line survival gear, middle ground prepping depends on gear and supplies that are of reasonable quality and will function properly during what is hoped to be a once in a lifetime emergency. Having some emergency supplies could make a bad situation more tenable, or it could save your life! While the government currently recommends enough supplies to support you for up to 72 hours (3 days), 14 days really should be your minimum for middle ground prepping.

Within a couple weeks, roads could be made accessible (not rebuilt, just accessible), rioting may subside, and commerce (food deliveries to stores) could start moving again. Most homes and even apartments should be able to easily store a couple weeks' worth of food supplies without building an underground bunker for storage. In fact, with the exception of some perishable items, the majority of households probably have a couple weeks' worth of food in their pantries and cupboards right now.

When planning your food supplies consider the fact that water and heat for cooking may be limited, or non-existent, post disaster. As such, work on identifying foods and products that you could (or be willing to) eat without heating and without adding water. If you do have a way to cook with heat and water that would be a bonus.

When planning emergency supplies for your pets make sure you have appropriate leashes or carriers within easy access to evacuate your animals out with you. You will also need at least a three day supply of food and water specifically for your pet and any medications that they may require on a daily basis. While there are some prepackaged pet emergency kits on the market they are very generic with standard size leashes and vacuum sealed food. A German shepherd would not be well controlled on such as thin leash, and probably would not eat any food that he is not used to on a daily basis unless starving. If your pet eats soft canned foods regularly, they would not do well with the hard kibble contained in these pre-packaged pet emergency kits. It is recommended that you to make your own evacuation kit specifically for your pet and include some of their normal food.

7. **Family meeting** – The fact that you have put together a good emergency plan is great, but does little if you and your family do not review it together. Once you have a written plan, sit down with the whole family and discuss every aspect of your plan. Encourage all to ask questions and make sure that if you have assigned specific roles to family members that they fully understand the importance of their role.

   A key element of this family meeting is NOT to scare the family and leave them living in fear of some impending doom. Education is the key to having the family understand probability and measured preparedness. Children are constantly doing homework to prepare themselves for upcoming quizzes and tests. Emergency preparedness is no different. When you neglect to study, you get poor grades. When you neglect to prepare for disasters, you make bad decisions which can put you in bad situations that could cause you harm. Middle ground prepping is all about improving family safety without being fanatical doomsday believers.

Remember, actions you take for personal preparedness will improve your mental readiness for disasters. Letting your family know that you have written emergency plans and emergency kits on hand also reassures them that you have resources to manage the event. This should assure most that they have some sense of control during an emergency. Knowing how to communicate and bring your family back together will soothe a lot of stress your family may feel.

8. **Vital documents** – While getting you and your family out of harm's way is always the first priority; some additional preparation can help make the recovery process after a disaster much easier. Managing your vital documents and having them readily accessible to you following a disaster will be a benefit. The amount of vital documents you have will depend upon your age, family size, insurance needs, and level of financial investments. This will be the least expensive preparation you have to accomplish.

   Regardless of the volume of documents practice the Backup 3-2-1 Rule. For all your critical financial and legal documents and records, make three copies, keep them in two different storage formats (for example, DVD, hard-drive, flash drive, remote server or cloud) and keep one copy away from your home (e.g., a safe deposit box or with a relative). With recent weather disasters affecting whole regions, you may even want to keep this copy with a trusted relative in another state. For a comprehensive listing of the types of

documents you could consider as your vital
documents see Table 1 below.

Table 1

Documents and Keys	(✓)
Personal identification (driver's license, ID cards, military ID, etc.)	
Current photos of individual family members and pets (scan to CD or flash drive)	
Cash and coins	
Credit/Debit cards, associated pin numbers and Customer Service numbers to cancel (if lost)	
Blank checks (so you can write checks to pay bills or buy items)	
Extra set of keys or copy of lock combinations (e.g., house, car, mailbox, safe deposit box, gun safe, PO box, gate locks, desks, auto spare tires, boats, RVs, storage sheds, etc.)	
Copies of the following:	
- Birth certificates	
- Marriage certificate	
- Death certificate(s)	
- Vehicle registrations, titles, bill of sales, proof of insurance	
- Social security card or naturalization or citizenship papers	
- Passports, Green cards and Military IDs	
- Adoption, custody or foster care records	
- Divorce records	
- Wills/Living trust contact (Never put the original of your will in a safe deposit box because if you die, the bank may seal it temporarily. Keep it with your lawyer, trusted family member or executor.)	
- Power of attorney, living will and advanced medical directives	
- Deed of Trust (or utility bill to prove residency)	
- Deed to cemetery plots and burial contracts	

- Diplomas, business licenses, professional registrations	
- Self-employed: business insurance policy numbers, incorporation papers, backup of accounting records.	
- Computer and Web site user names/passwords	
- Inventory of household goods (list or video)	
- Insurance policies (home, auto, life, animal) and agent contact information	
- Medical, dental, and immunization records	
- Prescriptions and doctor names	
- Membership cards	
- Bank savings, checking and ATM account numbers and Customer Service numbers to cancel (if lost)	
- Stock and bond certificates or investment/IRA/Roth account numbers (and contact phone numbers)	
- Employment benefit records, pension records (from current and previous employers)	
- Medicare, Medicaid, food assistance program records	
- Debts: what you are making payments on, how much and to whom.	
- Home security codes or electronic management apps/websites	
- Emergency contact list and phone numbers	
- Map of area, evacuation locations, and Family Communications Plan	
- Important contracts	

9. **Home Inventory** –While other emergency preparedness activities are much easier to accomplish like procuring go bags, making a complete home inventory of your belongings is much more labor intensive. However, a home inventory is an excellent way to expedite the insurance claim process after theft, damage, or loss from a disaster. Having a record of your insurable assets will not only help you in the

settlement of a claim, but will also help verify tax-deductible property losses and determine the right amount of insurance coverage you should have. Obviously, you need a list of what you own (or at least what you would like to replace), the manufacture, when the item was purchased (at least the approximate year) and its purchase price (not today's cost) or best estimate.

As part of your overall emergency preparedness plan, making your home inventory can be as simple as a written list with photos or a video record with descriptive narration of your belongings. You can easily make a spreadsheet of your assets broken down by rooms in your home including the garage, attic, and basement. Or you can utilize free applications provided by the major insurance companies. State Farm's HomeIndex is a free online tool that combines the home inventory list with a visual record, all in one place. HomeIndex makes documenting your valuables especially easy because it walks you through the inventory process and allows you to share your inventory with your agent. Allstate has their free Digital Locker application that allows you to keep an inventory of all your personal property and accessible to you at a moment's notice on your smart phone or any web-based device.

Aside from these company proprietary applications, there is a plethora of software applications available on the market to help in your emergency preparedness and creation of a home inventory. Most range from $10 to $50 and allow you to download video and photos in the application as well as detailed item descriptions. As with any worthwhile project, do not try and do your entire home on a Saturday afternoon. Do it a little at a time, maybe just one room a week and make sure you do a good job of documenting manufacturer names, serial numbers, models, approximate purchase date and cost. The more information you have the better.

This element of your preparedness plan is essential and the hours you spend creating and maintaining (perhaps on a monthly basis) this inventory will save you many more should disaster strike your home!

Acquiring

Once you have developed your emergency plan, it is time to start acquiring the supplies you will need to withstand the various threats that can affect you and your family. The types of supplies you will need were presented in detail in Chapter 5 and you can develop a long-term plan for procuring and storing your needed supplies. Obviously, this buying plan will depend upon your available funding and storage capability, but should still be done in a timely manner to meet your immediate readiness goals.

Water is the most critical emergency supply you will need and based on the Rule of 3's, you generally can only go three days without water at which point the human body starts to shut down, organs may fail, and you can die. Plan your water needs first!

Based upon your risk assessment, determine the number of days your family may need an emergency water supply. As previously mentioned there are several strategies for storing water that are readily available to you. You may start with cases of 500ml or litre plastic water bottles. These are easy to store and stackable. While many prefer larger litre storage bottles, the smaller the container the less water you will tend to drink. For a small family such water may be sufficient; however, larger families with increased daily water needs may opt for larger water storage options. These may include five gallon up to 55 gallon containers. Finding a good place to store such containers may be a problem so consider storage locations before you purchase these larger containers.

Assuming that you did not stockpile enough water you should always be able to purify some additional water if it did not come from your faucet. I recommend chlorine dioxide tablets that can kill viruses, bacteria and protozoa (including Giardia and Cryptosporidium).

In terms of food specifically, do not buy a thing until you have a good idea of how much food and water you are planning to store and where. A major mistake during the acquisition phase is to start buying stuff haphazardly and then realizing that you should have bought different items or different sizes to maximize your meal requirements and storage space.

Again, based on your risk assessment for your area, determine your initial goal for how many days of emergency food storage you want. First, prioritize your food and water items along with your planned quantities. Remember you will be eating three meals a day. Include any storage containers, shelving, or products you will need to store your supplies. Second, take an inventory of your current food supplies to see if you have any items that are required in your plan. If you find some, then you will not need to procure those items thereby saving money.

When considering your food supplies remember that during a power outage perishable foods in your refrigerator and freezer will be the first to spoil. Either have a plan for using a backup generator to provide electricity to keep the refrigerator running or eating the refrigerated and frozen foods first if possible before they spoil.

Remember also that you will need two types of food supplies. One will be the food items you keep in your emergency kits or go-bags, and the other will be those supplies you can keep at home for shelter-in-place emergencies. Acquiring supplies will be an ongoing process, because as mentioned earlier, you will need to actually consume some or your food supplies on a regular basis and they will need to be replaced and refreshed.

With a solid food and water supply plan in place, start working on the remaining emergency supply items such as first aid supplies, emergency lighting devices, portable radios, sanitation items, temporary shelter items, and communication items. Remember, when purchasing these items you must constantly evaluate quality vs. cost for these sparsely used items. Spending a small fortune on items that may never be used is not practical yet the items must be of sufficient quality to perform at least once in an emergency.

At this point, you can begin focusing on remaining emergency items such as first aid, lighting, communications, sanitation, and shelter items. An easy way to get the items you need may be to simply purchase commercial off-the-shelf emergency kits and go bags to meet your family's needs.

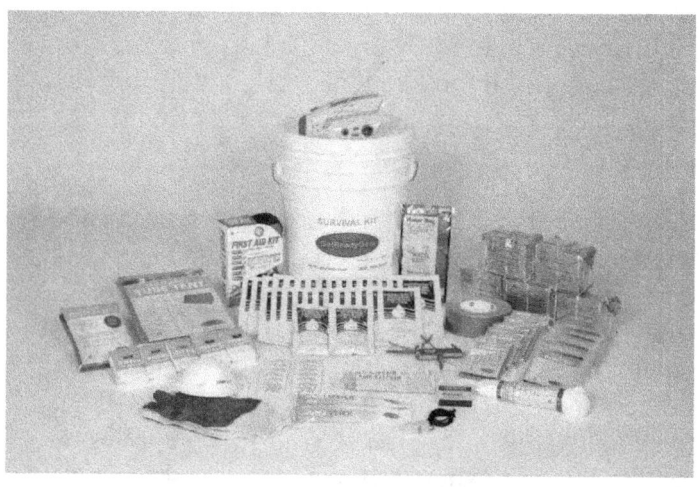

5 Person Home Emergency Kit

Responding

For any given emergency or disaster event there are really only two options available to you, shelter-in-place or evacuation.

Shelter-in-place – You should not, and will not have the time to seal off your entire home with plastic sheeting and tape as many people envision to shelter-in-place. A more middle ground prepping approach is to identify a safe room or rooms in your home.

When using the term "Safe Room" one can conjure up several different visions. First, there is the security safe room of 2002 Panic Room movie fame. Such rooms are designed to provide a safe place to await the arrival of police when intruders enter your home. Secondly, with all the recent tornado activity in the heartland, there are dozens of companies manufacturing and selling safe rooms (or storm shelters). Most of these are designed out of steel or concrete to withstand tornado force winds and they can be secured in your existing garage or built into a new home. Make sure that if you procure such as safe room that it meets FEMA's P-320 and P-361 specifications. Finally, the more simplistic definition of a "Safe Room" is a room in your home where you and your family can shelter-in-place with your home emergency kits.

Sheltering-in-place is a survival technique to protect persons from a severe weather event (tornado, etc.) or an environmental emergency (airborne hazardous material spill, biological agent, or radiological release) by staying indoors. This is a precaution aimed to keep you safe by staying indoors (this is not the same as going to an evacuation shelter).

Your "safe room" depends upon the type of home you live in and the type of shelter-in-place event. Home types include one story, multi-level, and homes with basements. As events can be weather related or airborne related you may actually have two different safe rooms identified in your plan. In either case, it is ideal to have your emergency kits in your safe room. However, if your safe room has no storage space, you should look for a storage spot on the way to your "safe" room, like a closet. This way any family member could collect the kit(s) on the way to the "safe" room.

Additionally, having a hard-wired telephone in your safe room in case cell phone structures are damaged and not providing service is optimum. You may be able to use this phone to call your emergency contact and advise them of your status. The phone could also be used to report a life-threatening condition and with 9-1-1 recognition first responders would know your location.

Safe Room location #1 would be for a severe weather event such as a tornado or high wind event that may necessitate you to shelter-in-place until the threat of dangerous weather has passed. In such instances, your safe room should be

- on the lowest level of your home which may be a basement or subterranean storm shelter on your property, if you have one;
- a small, interior room if possible, with no or few windows, or a hallway on the first floor;
- a FEMA F-5 certified storm shelter that was professionally installed.

Safe Room location #2 would be for an airborne environmental hazard such as a chemical, biological, or radiological release. For such an event, your safe room should be

- an interior room with few or no windows, or a hallway on the ground floor of your home. Many hazardous materials and chemicals are heavier than air which is why a basement is NOT recommended for such events.
- sealed using tape and plastic sheeting (heavier than food wrap) to seal all cracks around any door, openings, windows and vents in your safe room. You could also use a wet towel to stuff under a door to ensure complete sealing. Knowing what openings need to be sealed in your safe room will allow you to pre-cut your plastic sheeting and have it ready ahead of time. According to experts, a tightly sealed, 10' x 10' room will have enough oxygen to last one person for about five hours.

If you have time prior to entering your safe room

- close and lock all windows and exterior doors in your home;

- turn off all fans, heating, and air conditioning systems;
- close the fireplace damper if you have one;
- bring your pets with you, and be sure your emergency food and water supplies are in the room; and
- if your safe room is a fabricated storm shelter, make sure you understand how it is vented if you intend to use it during airborne environmental events.

Once you are in your safe room

- close the window shades, blinds, or curtains if you are told there is a danger of explosion;
- stay in the center of the room away from doors and windows; and
- listen to the Emergency Alert System on your emergency radio or TV until the "All Clear" signal is given or you are told to evacuate.

For those people who live in pre-manufactured or mobile homes, remember that your home is not the ideal place for a severe weather event safe room because of the inherent structural weakness in these units. As a result you should have a plan in place to seek shelter in a well-constructed building nearby or shelter. You can however, designate a safe room in such structures for an airborne environmental hazard.

Recently there has been significant interest and marketing regarding emergency bunkers. While the vast majority of home owners in the US do not have enough land to install an underground bunker, they also do not have the money! Do you really think your HOA will approve a bunker installation in your backyard?

However, there is a great deal of value in the much smaller tornado shelters now available for installation in your garage or built into a new home. These tend to be more affordable as you would only be in such a shelter for a couple minutes and probably less than a half hour. Therefore, there is no need for expensive ventilation, air purification, lighting, or sanitation systems. A simple flashlight and five gallon bucket toilet could work just fine in such a shelter. But the expense is probably not justifiable in areas not prone to tornadoes.

It is also possible that you would need to shelter-in-place at work or even in your car. Most large companies should have an emergency plan for its employees to shelter-in-place. But if your office is small you may need to be the one figuring out the best safe room in your office or building. Many consider their car survival kit to be used as an office kit as well, and this is fine if you can get to your car after the emergency. But keep in mind that a shelter-in-place emergency would generally not allow you access to your car in the parking lot.

If you happen to be in your vehicle and hear about a shelter-in-place order on the radio or see severe weather, you are generally better off staying in the relative safety of your vehicle. You would want to pull off the road in a safe manner, lock your doors, roll up all the windows and turn off your air conditioner or vent. However, a key exception to this rule is a tornado. Due to the dynamics of the high winds associated with a tornado, it is recommended to drive your car to the nearest structure or building and get inside for maximum protection.

Evacuation – When it is safer to move people out of the way of an impending danger, local law enforcement will issue an evacuation order. Depending upon the scope and urgency of the order, law enforcement will either be coming door-to-door or broadcasting notifications over speakers from patrol vehicles or helicopters. The Emergency Alert System should also be broadcasting the evacuation order.

The initial evacuation order may be "voluntary" but as the danger grows closer the evacuation will become "mandatory." Again, in order to effectively evacuate, do so when the "voluntary" evacuation order is announced. If you wait for the "mandatory" evacuation order you could get snarled in traffic heading out of town and potentially run out of gas as well.

Many folks believe that they will need a secondary shelter located some distance from their home in order to "ride out" various disaster scenarios. Again, the majority of people do not have access to such property and shelters such as an underground bunker, cabin, or vacation home. The concept of middle ground prepping would instead have you consider family or close friends whom you could stay with during a disaster evacuation from your home. Another good option for many Americans is to hit the open road with their RV and head to a location or to a family or friend's residence a safe distance away from the disaster zone.

Many fanatical preppers believe that they will need a bulldozer type vehicle to plow their way through or over unimaginable traffic jams on their way out of town. The traffic jams could be real especially if you do not evacuate at the first sign of trouble. Once local officials announce a mandatory evacuation, it could be too late! Make sure you evacuate well ahead of any coming disasters such as hurricanes, floods, and wildfires. Maintain at least one vehicle in such condition that it could make a 400-500 mile round-trip if needed. Keep your gas tanks full or store a little extra gasoline at the house.

Training

Many fanatical preppers, mostly those with previous military experience, believe in the need for heavy weaponry (and lots of it) and advanced self-defense training in order to survive hand-to-hand combat when the marauders come. I am not advocating selling your guns, nor avoiding that self-defense class on Wednesday evenings, but becoming an expert in Krav Maga and the need to mount a machine gun on your quad (as shown on Doomsday Preppers) is extreme. If you have weapons, being proficient with them is always a prudent idea. Do not go out and buy a pistol and a shotgun and then never go to the range and practice. Untrained owners can make guns dangerous.

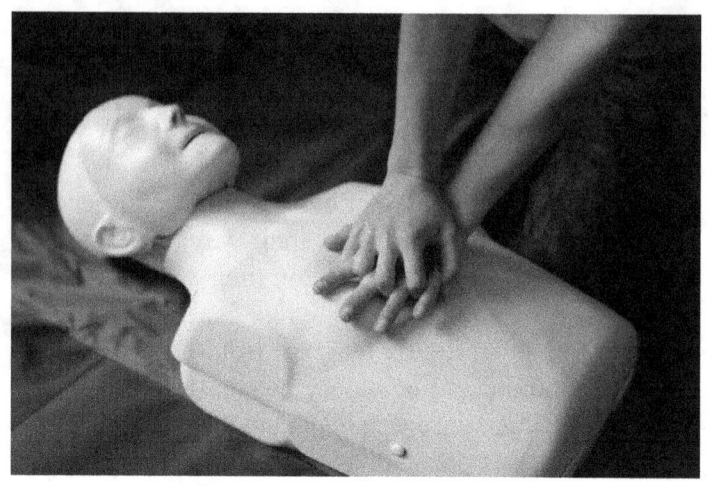

CPR training can save lives

Make sure you have at least some basic first aid training along with cardiopulmonary resuscitation (CPR). Being able to remediate minor disaster medical problems will be a significant skill when first responders are not available to assist you. Go out and find a local first aid and CPR class. Some communities offer these for free.

Managing three killers – In emergency medicine there are three basic situations that can kill you in a pre-hospital environment such as a disaster. While the procedures are not complicated, a little medical training could allow you to save the life of a family member or friend in an emergency. Many will remember the ABCs of how to save a life. Airway, Breathing and Circulation must be managed in this order. Your airway is the most important aspect of emergency medical operations. Without a viable airway, a person cannot survive. Secondly, the person must be able to continue to breathe on their own. Thirdly, they must have adequate blood circulation throughout the body to provide nutrition to all body parts and remove waste products effectively.

In emergency medicine, the three "killers" are

1. airway obstruction,
2. bleeding, and
3. shock.

Being able to control these three killers until emergency first responders can arrive after a 9-1-1 call, could make the difference between life and death for a family member or friend. The easiest way to learn such skills would be to take basic life support courses from the Red Cross or take an online course, IS-317 Introduction to Community Emergency Response Teams. Such courses will teach you how to open an obstructed airway for an unconscious person. Once the unconscious person has a clear airway, you will learn how to keep the airway open until help arrives.

One way to develop an obstructed airway is to be choking on something. You should also learn how to perform an abdominal thrust (which used to be called the "Heimlich Maneuver") to aid a choking victim. Studies show that 2800 people die each year by choking on food. Of these, most are children four years of age and under.

Once a person's airway is clear and they are breathing on their own, your next concern is bleeding. While bleeding may be visibly more dramatic, airway control must come first. In order to manage bleeding you will learn how direct pressure, elevation and pressure points will stop most injuries that are bleeding. You will also learn that often times, head injuries that are bleeding excessively due to the volume of capillaries in the head and face may not be that critical. Effectively managing bleeding can prevent hypovolemic shock (a loss of circulating blood volume) which leads us to our third killer.

Ultimately, the human body inevitably dies from some form of shock (e.g., anaphylactic, cardiogenic, neurogenic, etc.). Being able to remediate injuries and prevent the onset of shock will also buy you time until emergency first responders arrive. You need to learn how to recognize the signs and symptom of shock, so you can act quickly to counteract the mechanism of shock. Many will remember that raising a supine victim's feet above the heart will allow blood to flow back toward the trunk of the body where all of the critical organs are located. Having even these basic life support skills, could save a loved one or friend in an emergency. While it only takes a few hours to learn and be trained in these skills, it could provide a lifetime of peace of mind.

Stop thinking all this would be a good idea to know someday. Act now and improve your emergency preparedness capabilities by getting your family trained in basic life support skills; that may someday make a difference in someone's life.

Active shooter incidents – More and more we hear about "active shooter" events around the country. But not all such attackers use a gun which is why many are now starting to refer to such events more accurately as "active assailant incidents." According to the Department of Homeland Security (DHS), "An Active Shooter is an individual actively engaged in killing or attempting to kill people in a confined and populated area; in most cases, active shooters use firearms(s) and there is no pattern or method to their selection of victims." Obviously, the recent tragedy in Aurora, CO was an active shooter (James Holmes) event, as was the Virginia Tech massacre in 2007 by Seung-Hui Cho. Generally, the shooter has no specific target in mind; they just want to kill people for some twisted reason. Knowing how to react in such a situation could save your life.

The DHS actually has a guideline for an active shooter response during a shooting event and a 45 minute training video "IS-907 Active Shooter: What You Can Do." Watching this video and reading the DHS guideline will help you and your family react in the most appropriate way possible to prevent harm.

In 2014, the FBI released a report of active shooter incidents (many met the criteria for mass shootings, others presumably attempted mass shootings) in the United States, showing that the number of these events is on the rise. In the period from 2007 to 2013, active shooter incidents had seemingly skyrocketed when compared to the period from 2000 to 2006. "The findings establish an increasing frequency of incidents annually," the report states. "During the first 7 years included in the study, an average of 6.4 incidents occurred annually. In the last 7 years of the study, that average increased to 16.4 incidents annually."[1] The DHS "Active Shooter, How to Respond" guideline was first compiled in 2008 for retailers and mall operators. However, the guideline is applicable to offices and any public gathering place.

The essence of the active shooter response guide is to attempt to evacuate or hide, and if those options are not available disrupt the attack by distracting the shooter or "taking him out." Remember, when faced with this terrifying situation you will react based upon what you know. Knowing your options could cause you to freeze in place. This is definitely a moment in time when you must survive.

Critical information in the active shooter response guideline has to do with post event actions. This is especially critical once law enforcement arrives on scene. You are advised to drop all items from your hands and keep them visible to officers. Remember, they do NOT know who the shooter is right away. Given all of the people that can be in and around an active shooter event, officers need to carefully determine who the shooter is and who the victims are.

Signals to get you rescued – Another key area of preparedness training is how best to signal for help? If you are lost or find yourself in need of rescue in the outdoors, and you do not believe rescuers to be nearby, you first need to move to the largest available clear and flat area on the highest possible terrain that you can access. In daylight hours you can

1.   Use your available gear to create a signal on the ground; generally this could be

unnatural geometric patterns such as straight lines, circles, triangles, etc. This could be done with reflective thermal blankets or a bright orange tube tent, using rocks to keep them in place. You could also use available tools or sticks to clear away weeds to create similar patterns on the ground that would be visible form the air. Such techniques may also help you avoid starting a wildfire.

2. Build a smoky fire with waterproof matches to mark your location if the terrain is free from dry brush and weeds. While the international distress signal convention is three columns of smoke, this may be difficult to maintain by yourself, or you may not have access to enough fuel, so at least build one. Think about creating a color of smoke that contrasts with the background; dark smoke against a light background and vice versa. If you smother a large fire with green leaves, moss, or drops of water, the fire will produce white smoke. If you add a rag soaked in oil (from a vehicle) or a vehicle tire you will get black smoke.

3. Use a signal mirror, a polished metal drinking cup, your belt buckle, or any similar shiny object that will reflect the sun's rays toward a visible rescue aircraft or persons on the ground.

At night

4. Fire is your most effective visual means for signaling. Attempt to build three fires in a triangle. Again, this may be difficult to maintain by yourself, or you may not have access to enough fuel, so at least build one.

5. Use a flashlight to send an SOS signal (three short flashes followed by three long flashes followed by three short flashes (dot-dot-dot, dash-dash-dash, dot-dot-dot) to any passing low flying aircraft; or use a strobe light that flashes around 60 times per minute, but use sparingly as these lights are generally battery operated.

Regardless of your location, if you believe rescuers are close enough to hear you try the following:

6. Whistle using your tongue and teeth (if you are some of the fortunate few that can), or blow your emergency whistle in three distinct blasts then wait for a response from rescuers before repeating the sequence. While three blasts is a standard here in the U.S. other parts of the world use six blasts with a three blast response from rescuers. The international distress signal is six long blasts followed by a long silence. Most search and rescue teams are trained to listen for three blasts here in the U.S. You can also bang on pipes or make other similar noises using the pattern of three followed by silence. Try to use materials that will make more

noise than clapping hands; such as a rock, debris, belt buckle, or shoe, etc.

Your final option is to yell for "help"; however, you can blow a whistle a lot longer than you can yell for help. If you happen to be injured, yelling may actually hurt or your voice may be fainter than normal and difficult for rescuers to hear. So, remember to include signaling devices in your emergency kits.

Once the whole family knows what to do in an emergency, practice your escape routes and survival techniques together as if you were in a real emergency. Practice also possible evacuation routes, maybe one a month to ensure all family members are at least familiar with the routes and amenities along the way that may be useful, like gasoline. Most importantly, practice your first aid skills, as these are often lost within one month of initial training. You can pretend Dad has a broken arm and you need to splint it in a sling and swathe. Maybe one of the kids has a head laceration that needs bandaging. Be creative in your medical scenarios and over time try to include all your first aid skill sets.

Evaluating

Congratulations, you have finally completed your emergency plan, acquired needed supplies, practiced your escape and evacuation procedures and completed your first ever preparedness training class. Also remember to periodically evaluate your plans, supplies, and training needs.

It is generally recommended to evaluate your preparedness situation twice a year, when daylight savings time starts and when it ends. In general you should be considering the following changes:

- family changes,
- health changes,
- structural changes,
- environment changes,
- prescription changes/expire,
- food products expiring, and
- home inventory changes.

Families and their needs continually change

Family changes – While not an every year occurrence, your family may be expanding or contracting as life moves along. Newlyweds start a family, children are adopted, graduates head off to college, divorces occur and aging parents or college grads may move back in with you. Consider the number of persons in your household when evaluating the amount and types of supplies you have on hand. If changes are needed, add or subtract items as required. One final consideration here is that children grow! Be sure to keep current sizes of any supplies like gloves or other clothing.

Health changes – Many people completely forget to consider their family's changing health issues when evaluating their emergency supplies. For those on regular prescription or over-the-counter (OTC) medications, you should have a reasonable supply of their medications in your evacuation bags. This can be somewhat difficult to maintain as the family matures or a significant illness strikes a family member. Often times in addition to a large quantity of medications, you will have to deal with changing prescription strengths as illness progresses. Managing complex medication regimens requires a great deal of effort to ensure that you have a small supply of all the necessary medications, in the current dosage, that are NOT expired.

One of the easiest ways to do this is to have at least two 7 day pill containers will all the meds included. One will stay in your evacuation bag and one stays at home. Every time you renew a prescription, simply switch pill containers so that you use the almost expired pills (which have been in your evacuation bag) at home and your fresh pill container from the house would go into your evacuation bag.

You should also consider any medical supplies that are needed by a family member such as catheters, canes, hearing aids, diabetic testing supplies or a wheelchair.

Structural changes – If the square footage of your residence has increased or decreased, these changes should be evaluated relative to your storage capabilities and storage containers. Such changes could also have you re-thinking your escape/evacuation plans, where to keep your emergency supplies, where is your new safe room, and where to keep your evacuation bags?

Environment changes – Considering that you may have moved to a different climate could require you to modify your emergency supplies. Leaving California for Montana will most likely have you adding cold weather items to your supplies like stocking caps, gloves and hand warmers. However, if you are leaving the frigid north and heading to Arizona, you can probably store those cold weather items elsewhere in your home. Even if you are not moving to a different climate you may want to adjust your emergency supplies in the spring and fall to accommodate upcoming weather changes. No sense keeping those mittens in your kits as summer approaches.

Food products expiring – Depending upon your choice of food products in your emergency supplies, check them twice a year as well to ensure they are still "fresh." Many of the emergency high calorie food bars are good for up to five years, while MREs like Heater Meals are good for 18-24 months and freeze dried foods can be good for up to 20 years.

While water really never ever goes "bad," it can become stale and absorb odors from around the storage area. Depending upon what type of container the water is stored in, you may want to test at least one container when you evaluate your supplies to ensure it tastes fine.

Home inventory changes – And finally, remember that this is also a good time to check your home inventory and update it with any substantial purchases since your last evaluation. It is much easier to maintain this thorough list every so often than it is to update it after three or four years!

Summary

The concept of middle ground prepping allows for a measured and reasonable response to preparing for impending emergencies or disasters in order to protect yourself and your family. The components of a well thought out emergency plan can very simply mean the difference between life and death.

Considering your emergency planning as a group of small, well-defined steps will allow you to develop a comprehensive plan in a reasonable amount of time. By simply following the Planning, Acquiring, Responding, Training, and Evaluating steps you will experience considerable peace of mind and knowledge that your family is prepared to survive any disaster that may come your way. You can do it on your schedule without becoming obsessed with over-the-top preparedness notions and costs.

References:

1. Blair, J. Pete, and Schweit, Katherine W., *A Study of Active Shooter Incidents, 2000 - 2013*. Texas State University and Federal Bureau of Investigation, U.S. Department of Justice, Washington D.C., 2014.

Summary

Modern day prepping was born during the self-sufficiency days of the Great Depression, reinforced by our nation's war efforts and deeply rooted in religious beliefs. Most preppers today learned their skills from their parents and grandparents and continue to hand down the practices to their children. The "Millennials" will carry the middle ground prepping torch into the mid-21st century and the government will continue to try and figure out how to keep them motivated to prepare for the next disaster. But the U.S. has a way to go still with less than half the citizenry owning an emergency evacuation kit, and two thirds have no communication plan or emergency meeting place.

The concept of middle ground prepping allows for a measured and reasonable response to preparing for impending emergencies or disasters in order to protect yourself and your family. A well thought out emergency plan can very simply mean the difference between life and death. Middle ground prepping involves understanding the phases of any disaster and how you may react during each of those phases. Periodic training is a great way to continuously learn about disasters and prepare you for the mental and emotional challenges of a disaster.

Your preparedness activities will certainly be constrained by your available time, funding, and skills. However, at any level, middle ground prepping will guide you to procure appropriate supplies and create effective emergency plans. To gain acceptance of your plans, include the whole family in the discussion to promote family communication and responsibility at all ages.

Middle ground prepping is about doing it on your schedule without becoming obsessed with over-the-top preparedness notions and costs. It is the same process as saving money, losing weight, or getting in shape at the gym; you just have to start small and *prepare for the unexpected®*.

For those who can honestly say that they have done some emergency preparations, and those millions of Americans who have done no preparations at all, now is the perfect time to begin middle ground prepping. Simply follow the Planning, Acquiring, Responding, Training and Evaluating steps outlined in this book and you will experience considerable peace of mind and knowledge that your family is prepared to survive any disaster that may come your way. Take some personal responsibility, do not bet on the government bailing you out, and start middle ground prepping today.

We appreciate you taking the time to read this book and invite you to share your thoughts and reactions.

 https://www.goodreads.com/book/show/26143016-middle-ground-prepping

Jim Serre